Cobury Terrace
30 Nov 2015.

Dear Viviané.

Merry Christmas
2015.

enjoy

love P xxx

How to Believe

How to Believe

John Cottingham

B L O O M S B U R Y
LONDON · OXFORD · NEW YORK · NEW DELHI · SYDNEY

Bloomsbury Continuum
An imprint of Bloomsbury Publishing Plc

50 Bedford Square   1385 Broadway
London   New York
WC1B 3DP   NY 10018
UK   USA

www.bloomsbury.com

Bloomsbury, Continuum and the Diana logo are trademarks of
Bloomsbury Publishing Plc

First published 2015

© John Cottingham, 2015

British Library Cataloguing-in-Publication Data
A catalogue record for this book is available from the British Library.

Library of Congress Cataloguing-in-Publication data has been applied for.

ISBN: HB: 978-1-4729-0744-8
ePDF: 978-1-4729-0746-2
ePub: 978-1-4729-0745-5

2 4 6 8 10 9 7 5 3 1

Printed and bound in Great Britain by CPI Group (UK) Ltd, Croydon CR0 4YY

To find out more about our authors and books visit www.bloomsbury.com.
Here you will find extracts, author interviews, details of forthcoming events
and the option to sign up for our newsletters.

For MLC in love and gratitude

Contents

Foreword

Many people I meet express a strong interest in questions of religion and spirituality, but make it clear that they could not themselves become believers. Religious belief has ceased to be a live option for them. And it seems doubtful whether further intellectual analysis and argument would make much difference.

Bertrand Russell once observed that if he met God in the next world he would complain that God had not provided sufficient evidence of his existence. But there are other kinds of evidence than the kind studied by science. Many aspects of our experience (think of the dynamics of a loving relationship, or the appreciation of a complex piece of classical music) can only properly be apprehended by someone who is suitably receptive. A kind of 'attunement' is required; this in turn may require certain prior changes to have taken place in the subject – moral and aesthetic and emotional changes, for example. Where receptivity of this sort is involved, we are in a different domain from that of scientific inquiry.

This has led me to wonder whether many of those who might like to believe but cannot see their way to doing so may perhaps be looking in the wrong place. They may be looking for evidence offering the kind of security that a well-established scientific theory will provide, but they look in vain. So part of what I am aiming to do in this book is to indicate some alternative directions in which to look.

A religious worldview, if it is to be tenable at all, must not just engage our intellectual and scientific curiosity, but must take account of *all* the ways in which we respond to the world, including our emotional and imaginative modes of awareness. Philosophers in the past have often tended to discount these responses, preferring to take refuge in complex logical abstractions that put them at a certain superior distance from the phenomena they are supposed to be understanding. But such distance is achieved at a cost. It's almost as if there is a hypertrophy of the 'left-brain' skills, whereby we analyse and classify and dissect phenomena, without proper scope being accorded to the 'right-brain' skills that facilitate more intuitive and holistic forms of cognition.[1]

Allowing scope for our emotional and imaginative faculties most emphatically does *not* mean abandoning rationality. All our faculties are needed for the full flourishing of our humanity, and a belief system that is informed by all the different human modes of awareness does not thereby lose its claim to qualify as a rational and well-grounded system. I have elsewhere argued for the need for a 'humane' turn in philosophy, one that retains the rigour and precision for which the subject is rightly prized, but which aims to embrace all the aspects of our human awareness as we confront the world.[2] It is my hope that something of this 'humane' dimension may emerge in the course of the present book.

I am well aware that alongside those who might like to believe – if they could see their way to doing so – there are others who have no wish whatever to believe, and who may be sceptical, or even irritated, when they feel someone is trying to nudge them in that direction. I would certainly not presume to try to 'convert' such

---

[1] See Iain McGilchrist, *The Master and his Emissary* (New Haven: Yale University Press, 2009).

[2] John Cottingham, *Philosophy of Religion: Towards a More Humane Approach* (Cambridge: Cambridge University Press, 2014). See also http://www.closertotruth.com/contributor/john-cottingham/profile (accessed 18 April 2015).

readers – this is a work of philosophy, not of what is sometimes called 'apologetics'. But I hope that even those who are highly sceptical about the acceptability of religious belief may find some interest in the account of the dynamics of belief developed in the pages that follow. For if that account is on the right lines, religious belief may turn out to be less about advancing explanatory hypotheses to rival those of science than about ways of responding to certain deep psychological and moral features of our human predicament.

Many people in our contemporary climate have discarded religious belief for reasons that are entirely understandable, including being repelled by the dogmatism and exclusivism of some practitioners of religion and the blinkered, anti-scientific stance of others, not to mention the use of religion as a cloak for corruption or an excuse for violence. But despite all this, I am convinced there is much in the great religions that is immeasurably enriching to humankind, and that the kind of enrichment offered cannot easily be achieved in any other way. If we can get beyond the confrontational attitudes that are such a depressing feature of much current debate, perhaps some of these riches may be recovered.

Is this a task for philosophy? That will be for the reader to judge, in the pages that follow. But I will just add that in my view philosophy cannot ultimately thrive if it collapses into a host of isolated academic specialisms, hedged in by walls of impenetrable jargon that keep out all but the 'experts'. It needs to break out of the confines of learned technical debate and recover its continuity with the rest of our intellectual culture, and with the great traditions, including the religious traditions, that have, whether we like it or not, shaped so much of our thinking. Philosophy at its best has always striven to achieve a 'synoptic' vision of reality, a 'worldview' that, so far as possible, aims to make sense of the cosmos and of our human place within it.

In charting the path towards belief I am conscious of how much I have learned from others, and it is no mere perfunctory expression of humility to acknowledge how much I still have to learn. But I shall be happy if the reflections that follow at least do something to rescue the topic of religious belief from sterile polemics between entrenched supporters and implacable opponents, and to bring into view how wrestling with such questions is not just a debating exercise, but one that engages deep sensibilities and longings that all human beings share.

I have been most fortunate to have benefited from many enriching exchanges with colleagues at lectures, conferences and seminars during the past few years, during which the ideas developed in this book were shaped, and many influences will be obvious in the pages that follow. I should just here like to record my special thanks to Fiona Ellis, Clare Carlisle and David McPherson for kindly reading and commenting on earlier versions of the typescript. I am also most grateful to Robin Baird-Smith for his help and encouragement.

West Berkshire, England
March 2015

Chapter 1

Contrasting visions

> *For starry night remains not long*
> *for mortals, nor doth wealth, nor care,*
> *but in a moment they are gone,*
> *and soon upon another comes*
> *the share of joy and sorrow.*
>
> Sophocles[1]

1. The onset of autumn

In *The Fifth Woman*, one of the series of *Wallander* novels by the acclaimed Swedish crime writer Henning Mankell, the troubled and depressive protagonist, Inspector Kurt Wallander, broods over the onset of autumn.

> A mouse scurried past his feet and vanished behind an old clothes chest that stood close to the wall. It's autumn, thought Wallander. The fieldmice are finding their way into the walls of houses. It will be winter soon.[2]

---

[1] Sophocles, *The Women of Trachis* [430 BC], trans. J. C.
[2] Henning Mankell, *The Fifth Woman* [*Den femte kvinnan*; 1996], trans. Steven T. Murray (New York: Vintage Crime, 2004), p. 172. The wording quoted above is from the translation given by John Lingard, to whose insightful article 'Kurt Wallander's Journey into Autumn' (*Scandinavian–Canadian Studies* 17 [2006–7], 104–5) I am greatly indebted.

Gloomy apprehension about the oncoming of the long Nordic
winter is a familiar theme in Scandinavian literature, but
Wallander's angst is more than climatic or geographical. The
impending bleakness of winter can be seen as a symbol of the
threatened descent of society into lawlessness, as the veneer of
Swedish order and civility cracks open to reveal a dark underworld
of violence. And caught in this changing world, where the old
certainties are being eroded, Wallander has a sharp sense of his
own transience and vulnerability, 'a pathetic figure, a policeman in
much too thin clothing, struggling against the wind in a desolate
Swedish town in autumn'.[3]

There is a universality here. All of us 'struggle against the wind',
and the chill of the turning year tells us of the 'chances and changes
of this mortal life' and our eventual inevitable extinction in the
winter of death. The ancient Romans, in the story of Proserpina,
daughter of Ceres, the crop goddess, lamented on how even the
beauty of spring and the vigour of youth are hostages to Dis, the
dark Lord of the underworld. And the poet John Milton evokes
this story when he speaks of the curse of our mortality, and
laments the Paradise we have lost, which surpassed in beauty

> ... that faire field
> Of *Enna*, where *Proserpin* gathring flours,
> Herself a fairer flour, by gloomy *Dis*
> Was gatherd, which cost *Ceres* all that pain
> To seek her through the World ...[4]

When our thoughts turn to such themes of separation, bereavement
and death (and no human being can avoid it from time to time)

[3] Mankell, *The Fifth Woman*, p. 196; trans. Lingard (see previous note).
[4] John Milton, *Paradise Lost* [1674], ed. H. Darbishire (London: Oxford University
Press, 1958), Book IV, lines 268–72.

we are gripped by a cold shudder. Philosophers hold forth about 'existential angst' in all manner of complicated ways, but they are really only finding labels for what is there, lurking beneath the surface consciousness of even the most secure and well-adjusted human being: the fear of pain and loss and final annihilation, and the knowledge that in a certain sense, however fortunate we may be in our friends and loved ones, we will have to face these things alone. As the poet Rainer Maria Rilke says in his own reflections on the onset of autumn:

> He who has no house cannot build one now.
> Who now is lonely, lonely long must stay ...
> and up and down the empty streets will go
> restlessly roaming, as the dark leaves hound him.[5]

Yet for all that, there is another, very different, way of experiencing the autumn. The turning year can be seen not as the herald of winter and loneliness, but as the time of harvest, the time of fruition and plenty. In John Keats' famous ode, autumn is the 'season of mists and mellow fruitfulness', conspiring with the sun to 'bless' the vine with fruit, and to 'bend with apples the mossed cottage trees'.[6] The predominant tone is one of tranquillity, of attunement with the warmth and beauty of the world, a calm and joyful acceptance of the gifts of nature.

How can a single season of the year evoke such contrasting human reactions?

---

[5] *Wer jetzt kein Haus hat, baut sich keines mehr. / Wer jetzt allein ist, wird es lange bleiben ... / und wird durch den Alleen hin und her / unruhig wandern, wenn die Blätter treiben.* Rainer Maria Rilke, Herbsttag ['Autumn Day', 1902], trans. J. C. For a fuller discussion of this poem, see John Cottingham, *Philosophy of Religion: Towards a More Humane Approach* (Cambridge: Cambridge University Press, 2014), ch. 6.

[6] John Keats, 'Ode to Autumn' [1819].

2. An ambiguous world

The reason why humans can respond in such very different ways to the world around them is not far to seek. We know that our human situation is a profoundly ambiguous one, beset on the one hand by fragility, danger, the urgent needs of survival and the ever-present threat of mortality, yet at the same time furnished with unspeakably wondrous resources for the enjoyment and enrichment of life. The 'garden of Eden' story (if we are prepared to delve below the crude level of a literal–historical construal) says something profoundly true about our situation. It speaks of the flaws in our nature and the spectre of mortality that haunts us; yet it also tells us that in a certain sense we humans have been given all that we need – all things have been 'framed for our delightful use', as Milton puts it. The planet that is our home is indeed a world of spectacular beauty, an amazing, shimmering blue orb of light and life, enough to make any cosmic travellers weep for wonder if they should come upon it after countless eons of journeying across the empty wastes of space, having hitherto found nothing but boiling infernos and icy rocks. We do not know, and perhaps will never know, but it is just possible that of all the innumerable worlds in the galaxy, and perhaps even in the entire cosmos, ours is the one single world where life and thought has arisen. And it is a world of enormous fecundity and richness and diversity, supplying us with countless delights.

In the opening chapter of the Genesis story, God looks upon the entire world he has made and sees that it is *good*. The *Monty Python* team, in their comic parody of the Victorian hymn 'All things bright and beautiful', try to argue otherwise:

> All things dull and ugly,
> All creatures short and squat,
> All things rude and nasty,
> The Lord God made the lot.

Each nasty little hornet,
Each beastly little squid,
Who made the spiky urchin?
Who made the sharks? He did.[7]

There's something here of the precocious schoolboy, forced to attend chapel each morning, but delighted at his cleverness and sophistication as he sneers at the naivety of the school chaplain and the rest of his teachers. But in fact the mockery falls flat. As anyone knows who has leafed through the *National Geographic* magazine or watched a David Attenborough nature film, hornets and squids and sea urchins and sharks are all spectacularly wondrous creatures, intricate and beautiful of their kind. In reality, it is extraordinarily difficult to point to any part of the natural world that is intrinsically ugly; if we are searching for true 'nastiness' and 'beastliness' in the world, the prime candidates are the products of human greed and folly and exploitation: the mile upon mile of barbed wire fencing in the Middle Eastern semi-deserts, strewn with plastic rubbish bags flapping in the wind; the vast, stagnant floating island of waste, hundred of miles across, that pollutes the Pacific Ocean; the ever-expanding acres of ugly and dispiriting concrete spreading across the over-populated cities of Asia and many other parts of the globe. We may well agree with the words of another nineteenth-century hymn: 'every prospect pleases, and only man is vile'.[8]

To say the natural world is good and beautiful is not to say that it always affords a comfortable environment for any given species. All creatures living on the earth are obliged in a certain sense to work for their living, and we know that the wondrous variety

---

[7] From a 1980 *Monty Python* album; the verses are a parody of the hymn 'All things bright and beautiful' from *Hymns for Little Children* by Mrs Cecil Alexander (1848).

[8] From the hymn 'From Greenland's icy mountains' (1819) by Reginald Heber.

of species we observe has been shaped in large part by fierce competition for survival. We know too that the microbes and other rapidly mutating organisms that are part of that seething biosphere, and on which we depend for life, can often take dangerous disease-producing forms. We also know that the planet itself is not a tame and cosy place, but a fiercely dynamic macro-system that can produce cataclysmic eruptions and collisions, fires and floods, with often devastating results for ourselves and other life forms.

In short, our world is a world of continuing stress and challenge and threat. But it is also a world of enormous wonder and beauty, a beauty that, once we leave the confines of our cities, is so immediately and vividly present to us that no one, not even the sniggering *Monty Python* writers, can in integrity deny it, or refuse to be moved by it. The upshot is that our human condition, our human predicament, presents us with a crucial question. As human beings, living in a beautiful and good yet also a frightening and challenging cosmos, we have to decide how, as it were, to *comport* ourselves towards it. Is our orientation to be one of affirmation and hope, or is it to be one of revulsion and despair? Is it to be the vision of Joseph Conrad in the first of the passages that follow, or the vision described by Jonathan Edwards in the second?

Here, firstly, is Conrad, who in a letter to a friend compares the inexorable and grim processes of the natural world to a monstrous knitting machine, which has 'evolved itself out of a chaos', and which will eventually destroy everything, including mankind:

The most withering thought is that the infamous thing has made itself; made itself without thought, without conscience, without foresight, without eyes, without heart. It is a tragic accident – and it has happened. You can't interfere with it. It knits us in and it knits us out. It has knitted time, space, pain, death, corruption, despair and all the illusions – and nothing matters.[9]

In the climax of Conrad's best-known novel *The Heart of Darkness* (1899), the narrator Charles Marlow tells of his travels far up river in the Belgian Congo to a trading station where scenes of devastation and slaughter awaited him, and he found a dying company agent, Mr Kurtz, whose last words to him were 'The horror, the horror!' But the horror that the reader is invited to share encompasses far more than the violence of the African jungle or the greed and cynicism of the colonial exploiters. In a sense the whole world is, for Conrad, a horror, as is all too apparent from the vision of the universe as a blind, purposeless machine spewing out and then destroying everything – a universe where 'nothing matters'.

Here, by contrast, is the eighteenth-century American philosopher and theologian Jonathan Edwards, describing a formative experience he had when he was around twenty or twenty-one years of age:

> I walked abroad alone, in a solitary place ... and looking upon the sky and the clouds, there came into my mind so sweet a sense of the glorious majesty and grace of God, as I know not how to express ... After this, the appearance of everything was altered: there seemed to be, as it were, a calm, sweet cast or appearance of divine glory in almost everything. God's excellence, his wisdom, his purity and love, seemed to appear in everything, in the sun, moon and stars, in the clouds and blue sky; in the grass, flowers and trees, in the water and all nature ...[10]

---

[9] Joseph Conrad, letter of 20 December 1897, in *Joseph Conrad's Letters to R. B. Cunninghame Graham*, ed. C. T. Watts (Cambridge: Cambridge University Press, 1969), p. 56.

[10] From a memoir of 1723, reprinted posthumously in Jonathan Edwards, *A Treatise Concerning Religious Affections* (Philadelphia: Crissy, 1821), p. xxv.

If most people were asked which state of mind they would, other things being equal, prefer to be in for a prolonged period of time – that of Conradian horror, or the calm sweet joy felt by Edwards – it would not be much of a contest. But of course it is not as simple as that. One cannot simply decide to adopt a certain world picture because it is more heartening or less frightening. Belief is not a kind of voluntary choice, as if one could choose to accept one vision rather than the other in the way one can decide to turn right or left when going on a walk. All sorts of complicated assessments and background assumptions are involved in accepting or rejecting a certain vision of reality. Nevertheless, part of what is involved as we reflect on the world we live in is a kind of choice, a decision about how (to use the term introduced a moment ago) we should 'comport' ourselves towards the world. Let us try to understand this notion a little better.

3. Belief and comportment

The world confronts us with an ambiguous face, and, as we have seen, what people see as they look out at their surroundings can evoke very different responses. It may seem that how we react to things is a matter of a spontaneous upwelling of feeling, and that we do not have much control over it. But that is only partly true. Even animals, as the philosopher René Descartes pointed out, can be trained so that their initial reactions can be modified: a dog, naturally inclined to bolt at the sound of gunfire, can be trained to freeze, and then to run forward and fetch the partridge or the pheasant once the hunter has brought it down.[11] And if creatures devoid of language and discursive rationality can be got to modify their impulses, how much more ought we – who have the power of standing back from our surroundings and reflecting

---

[11] René Descartes, *Passions of the Soul* [*Les passions de l'âme*, 1649], art. 50.

on them – to be able to do the same for ourselves? Buddhist sages have advocated methods enabling us to detach ourselves from the immediate impact of the senses and the desires, suggesting, for example, that lustful attraction can be counteracted by reflecting on repulsive aspects of the body such as the entrails beneath the skin. The object of such an exercise is not to engender disgust, but rather to neutralize damaging cravings and foster an attitude of calm mindfulness and detachment.[12]

The basic idea here is that although the reality around us often seems to threaten our wellbeing, then even if we may not be able to alter the way things are, we may at least be able to change ourselves and our outlook. Variations on this idea inform much of Buddhist thinking, as well as ancient Hellenistic philosophies such as Stoicism, which influenced Descartes. Descartes is an interesting figure in this respect, since he was one of the pioneers of modern, mathematically based scientific thinking, and he foresaw how this new style of knowledge might be put to the service of humankind, improving our lot and freeing us from 'innumerable maladies both of body and mind, and perhaps even from the infirmities of old age'.[13] But as he grew older he came to have doubts about this aggressive strategy of conforming the world to our will by the power of the new science and technology, and instead he resigned himself to the Stoic expedient of resolving to change oneself by subduing the passions: 'Instead of finding ways to preserve life, I have found another much easier and surer way, which is not to fear death.'[14]

From these examples we glimpse the outlines of at least two of the ways in which humans may comport themselves towards the world. There is the modern scientific–technological route of

---

[12] See Nyanaponika Thera, *The Heart of Buddhist Meditation* [1954], ed. S. Boorstein (San Francisco: Weiser, 2014).

[13] Descartes, *Discourse on the Method* [*Discours de la méthode*, 1637], part vi.

[14] Descartes, Letter to Chanut of 15 June 1646.

'command and control', energetically taking charge of our bodies and our environment and endeavouring to alter them in whatever ways will ameliorate our human predicament. And there is the more ancient mode of quiescence and detachment, fortified (as in Buddhism) with certain time-honoured methods of liberating ourselves from our cravings and our dissatisfactions through the right kind of mindful meditation.

These two very different modes of 'comportment' towards the world are clearly not simply conditioned patterns of behaviour or mere utilitarian techniques; they involve a complex array of attitudes and beliefs about the nature of reality, and so may be thought of as having something in common with religious outlooks. Indeed, Buddhism is normally classified as a religion, and people sometimes speak of the modern scientific outlook as a kind of 'religion', meaning that many people put their faith in science as our best resource for understanding the world and dealing with the problems and puzzles of human life.

Nevertheless, both the Buddhist and the modern science-oriented modes of comportment are relatively 'light' on doctrine, at least when compared with theistic religions, such as the three great Semitic monotheisms, Judaism, Christianity and Islam. In Buddhism, for example, there is no personal deity; on the contrary, reality is taken to be an impersonal flux of conditions that arise and pass away. The fact that there is no need for a Buddhist to subscribe to the idea of a personal creator, and no need to regard the universe in a teleological light (as moving towards some ultimate destiny or purpose), may be one reason why it has considerable appeal for many Western intellectuals in our contemporary culture. The Buddhist vision is one that seems fully compatible with modern science's rejection of purposive explanations and its adoption of an explanatory schema in which phenomena arise through deterministic or probabilistic processes operating entirely without reference to humankind and its wellbeing.

It seems clear, then, that one may put one's faith in the Buddhist detached mode of comportment, or in the methods of modern scientific inquiry and technological control, without in either case having any quasi-religious beliefs about the ultimate goodness of the cosmos, and without subscribing to any idea that our salvation lies in our aligning ourselves with some ultimate reality. Critics of theistic religion may see this as a signal advantage: it shows that there are systematic and widely accepted ways of comporting oneself towards the world that do not require any controversial and hard to establish assumptions about a supreme being or deity, or about ultimate cosmic goodness, but which simply require us to view ourselves as part of the natural world and to live with it as best we may, whether drawing on the resources of modern science or cultivating the techniques of meditation and detachment.

Such alternatives to theism may also seem to offer a way of resisting the choice posed by the two opposing reactions to the world expressed by Conrad and Edwards respectively in the passages quoted in the previous section. Instead of viewing the world with revulsion and horror, as Conrad does, or as transfigured with divine glory, as in Edwards, we now seem on the face of it to be presented with a much calmer, more down-to-earth and more rational suggestion: the world is neither an intrinsically implacable mechanism, nor is it intrinsically glorious and divine, it simply *is* – neither good nor bad, but simply *there*. We can do what we can to understand and control it, or we can do what we can to escape suffering its effects as far as possible through calmness and detachment. But no more than this (on the argument we are now considering) should be expected or required. There are, on this view, no magical or mystical solutions from on high, and there is no heavenly destination where all will be made right. By attending to the world as it is, we may still have hard struggles in front of us, but at least, so runs this line of thought, we will not be resorting to comforting self-delusions. By comporting ourselves, clear-sightedly, in a way that is appropriate to the inhabitants of a godless, purely natural universe, we will have our best chance of living in a dignified and rational way.

There is much that is appealing in such a vision – indeed, in one form or another it clearly attracts a very large and perhaps growing number of people today. It would be absurdly arrogant for a theistic believer to try to claim that a life lived in accordance with such a vision cannot be a decent human life. What is more questionable, however, is the assumption that such a vision is a more realistic or a more clear-sighted one than the theistic alternative.

To begin with, assessing how rational or clear-sighted a given worldview may be depends on a host of background assumptions, not all of which are straightforward matters of fact. For example, the belief that we can improve things through scientific progress may seem to have much evidence in its favour (think merely of the significant reduction in human distress produced by, say, advances in dentistry, without even beginning to enumerate the more major life-saving achievements of modern medical science); but nevertheless there is a great deal of research indicating that beyond a certain basic threshold of comfort and physical security levels of human happiness do not continue to rise in tandem with advances in scientific and technological progress. Inspector Wallander, with whom we began this chapter, belongs to one of the most technologically and scientifically advanced cultures in history, yet he is no less prone to existential angst: the restlessness and disquiet that is the signature of our humanity remains. To suppose that *this* could be allayed by further advances in science and technology looks like an act of faith rather than a piece of pure, clear-sighted rationality. By the same token, believing that the path of Buddhist meditation offers the hope of ultimate bliss or enlightenment, the state known as Nirvana, must again be to some extent a matter of faith for someone setting out on such a path;[15] and even on a more immediate level, the strategy of freeing ourselves from attachment, though it may reduce the pain of disappointment and loss, is not obviously compatible with the deep-seated human impulse to commit ourselves to others that is arguably the key, albeit fragile, to our greatest happiness. So again, and however you evaluate these particular bits of the argument, the upshot seems to be that there is more to the adoption of a worldview than reason or logic or evidence alone. None of us can avoid having to decide how to comport ourselves towards the world, but there is no simple algorithm or formula for arriving at the right decision.

4. Transformation and truth

The discussion so far has oversimplified things in at least one important respect. It has assumed that we confront the world – a world that has such-and-such features – and that in the light of how those features present themselves to us we have to decide how to conduct ourselves towards it. But humans are not just passive observers of the world; we constantly interact with it. That much is true even of non-human animals. Yet in our human case there is an additional aspect, a kind of creative dimension. Instead of merely processing the data from the five senses in ways determined by the innate structure of our sense organs and nervous systems and shaped by our previous perceptions, humans have additional faculties, active creative powers of reflecting on and interpreting their experience. A group of children exploring a garden will not simply map it out and find their way around, but will, even from a very young age, transform it creatively into a rich locus of imaginative play, places to hide, scary dark corners to

---

[15] See Michael McGhee, *Transformations of Mind* (Cambridge: Cambridge University Press, 2000).

avoid, bushes that are 'monsters' to be confronted, banks that are places of safety and refuge.

The sober rationalist may dismiss this as 'mere imagination', or may take a more functional approach, talking of play as a useful mechanism that affords practice in learning to deal with what will later be the practical hazards of adult life. But far more is involved than that. In virtue of our unique conceptual powers and sensibilities, all of us do much more than encounter the world; we transform it, creating out of the raw data of perception a whole rich 'lifeworld', a world full of meaning and value. In other words, in our basic relation to the world there is, in the human case, a kind of *poetry*, in the strict etymological sense of *poēsis*, a 'making'. What the Nobel Laureate Seamus Heaney discusses in the following passage in reference to his own literary activity as a poet applies in a wider sense to the entire transformative relation in which human beings stand to the world:

> In order that human beings bring about the most radiant conditions for themselves to inhabit, it is essential that the vision of reality which poetry offers should be transformative, more than just a printout of the given circumstances of its time and place. The poet who would be most the poet has to attempt an act of writing that outstrips the conditions even as it observes them.[16]

Because we often think of imaginative writing as 'fiction', it is easy to misunderstand the point being made here as the banal claim that human beings have the capacity to 'make things up'. Much literary output is indeed fictional, in the sense that it does not record historical occurrences or consist of literal factual propositions.

---

[16] Seamus Heaney, 'Joy or Night' [1993], in *Finders Keepers: Selected Prose 1971–2001* (London: Faber, 2002).

But Heaney's point about human beings bringing about the 'most radiant conditions for themselves to inhabit' is a much more subtle and important one than that. Part of what he is saying is that the writer never produces a mere 'printout of given circumstances'. Indeed, on reflection it is clear that we cannot really grasp what such a raw 'printout' would be: there can never be, for humans, an uninterpreted world, a world that is not always already a world of significance, a world where some features are salient because of what they mean for us, and the way they point beyond themselves to other elements of our lifeworld.

The key concept at work here is not 'fiction' in the sense of making up things that are literally false, but *transformation*. When Heaney says that poetry should have a 'transformative' function, he does not mean that it distorts or alters things, changing a given item into something else. What the poet deals with, as the passage makes clear, is the real world: he has a 'vision of *reality*'. It is a vision that sharply embraces and delineates what is there in view, disclosing its significance. Poetry is thus not fiction, but *truth*, truth in the sense the German philosopher Martin Heidegger referred to when he harked back to the etymology of the Greek word for truth, *alētheia*, literally an 'unconcealment', a disclosing of what is (partly) hidden.[17]

Thinking more about Heaney's idea of a 'transformative vision', we can see that it has application far beyond the literary domain. When humans interpret the world, as they necessarily must, what happens is a kind of co-operation between the reality that is there before them and their own attempt at understanding it. And that is never a final and completed process; by its nature it engages the restlessness of the human search for meaning. So again, when Heaney talks of the poet's writing 'outstripping the conditions even

---

[17] Martin Heidegger, *Being and Time* [*Sein und Zeit*, 1927], trans. J. Macquarrie and E. Robinson (New York: Harper & Row, 1962), §219.

as it observes them', we can see something of the elusive mystery of Being (a topic to which we shall return in the next chapter). The nature of reality is never finally packaged up and definitively presented to us, and we always reach beyond the given in our human struggle to understand it.

The restlessness and the struggle that are inevitably involved here again mark a contrast between us and the other animals. For them, the world is 'given' in a relatively determined and fixed way; they are not confronted with a mystery of being, because they are simply wholly absorbed in dealing with it in ways directly related to their immediate needs. In this sense, they are 'at home' in the world, in a manner we can never be – a point powerfully underlined by Rilke in his *Duino Elegies*:

> *und die findigen Tiere merken es schon,*
> *das wir nicht sehr verläßlich zu Haus sind*
> *in der gedeuteten Welt.*

> [and the resourceful beasts notice quite soon
> that we are not very securely at home
> in the interpreted world.][18]

Once we have got this far, it is possible to see that a purely science-based vision of the world can never be a neutral way of describing what is 'given'. Rather, it is one particular way of dealing with reality – a way that involves a deliberate decision to filter out the interpreted world of meaning and value in favour of certain structural and quantitative descriptions that are suitable for the purposes of explanation and prediction. This is not at all to disparage science, whose achievements have been

---

[18] Rainer Maria Rilke, *Duino Elegies* [*Duineser Elegien*, 1923], First Elegy, trans. J. C.

enormous; nor, in itself, does it refute the type of worldview we were considering in the previous section, according to which concentrating on the methods of science is taken to offer the best and surest way for humans to improve their lives. But at the very least it opens the way for the possibility of alternative visions of reality, which cannot be dismissed as mere 'flights of imagination' or 'fiction', but which have a right to be considered as potential disclosures of the meaning of the world we inhabit. Theistic belief, belief in a personal Being who is the ultimate ground underlying the mystery of being in the universe and the source of its meaning and value, is just such a vision, a transformative vision that brings into salience features of the world that simply drop out of view in the quantitative printouts of particle interactions, or in the Buddhist-style conception of reality as an impersonal flow of conditions that arise and pass away, leaving our own deepest individuality and selfhood as nothing more than an illusion.

With this in mind, we can bring this chapter to a close by recapitulating the contrasting visions of autumn with which we began. For Mankell, the season is the bleak herald of winter and death; for Keats the mellow fruition of summer. We can of course recognize truth in both understandings, and hence perhaps in the end they both serve merely to bring home to us the ambivalence of the natural world we inhabit, and our perpetual human condition of oscillating between joy and sadness, hope and despair. But for the theist, there is more to say. For it is time to notice that the 'transformative vision' that is at the heart of a theistic worldview is not simply a vision of sweetness and light, as in Jonathan Edwards' touching but in some ways one-sided vision of a world infused with a 'calm sweet cast' of divine glory. The vision is more disturbing than that, as Rilke reminds us earlier on in his First Duino Elegy, where he cries out '*das Schöne is nichts als des Schrecklichen Anfang*' – 'beauty is nothing but the beginning of terror'. The divine power is a power beyond all final comprehension, a beauty that, in Rilke's words, 'serenely refrains from annihilating us'.[19]

Rilke's own particular views on the ultimate nature of reality are a matter of debate, but if we look at orthodox mainstream theism, it is clear that, properly understood, it is most emphatically *not* a bland, comforting vision of the kind that countless critics assume it to be. The Brazilian-born writer Roberto Unger in a recent book dismissively discards traditional theistic religion by referring to the irreparable flaws in the human condition, which he says religion tries to deal with by telling us 'everything is ultimately all right'. 'But everything is not all right', Unger continues, as if this is the clinching objection.[20] Yet in fact even a cursory scrutiny of the canonical texts of the great religions, certainly those of the Judaeo-Christian tradition, speak almost continually of the weakness and failure and vulnerability of the human condition. The transformative vision that is offered is not (despite the common caricature) the promise of a rosy world where everything is made good. Biblical writings, of course, include 'eschatological' passages, which speak of the 'last things', or the end of the world (though these are by no means as pervasive as is often imagined); yet on examination these passages never invoke cosy solutions, but on the contrary focus on fearful acts of confrontation and final judgement (as a glance at the Book of Revelation, for example, will make all too clear).

But the significance of such eschatological passages has in any case to be understood in the light of what is undoubtedly the central and predominant theme throughout the Judaeo-Christian (and indeed Islamic) Scriptures – a theme that has direct implications for this world and for how we are to live in it now. The vision is

---

[19] '*es gelassen verschmäht, uns zu zerstören*'; *Duino Elegies*, First Elegy.
[20] Roberto Mangabeira Unger, *The Religion of the Future* (Cambridge, MA: Harvard University Press, 2014), p. 1.

of a personal God who makes the most uncompromising moral demands upon us; where human beings are stretched to the limit; and where comfort and welfare lag in importance far, far behind the imperative to transform our wasteful and selfish lives and bring them into conformity with the goodness and justice where our true fulfilment lies.

How it is possible to move towards accepting such a vision will be addressed in later chapters. But the transformation offered by the theistic vision is not a transformation that makes reality a cheery and stress-free place, but one which opens up the possibility that we *ourselves* can be transformed, not by withdrawing from the world, or renouncing its demands and attachments, but by confronting our faults and seeking the grace to overcome them. And this is why the true expression of the theistic vision is not Mankell's gloomy fear of autumnal decay, nor Keats's romanticized vision of tranquil ripeness, but a very different kind of harvest – the painful, hard-won harvest of 'all times and seasons' described so powerfully by John Donne in a homily delivered on the evening of Christmas Day almost 400 years ago:

He can bring thy summer out of winter, though thou have no spring; though in the ways of fortune, or understanding, or conscience, thou have been benighted till now, wintred and frozen, clouded and eclipsed, damped and benumbed, smothered and stupefied till now, now God comes to thee, not as in the dawning of the day, not as in the bud of the spring, but as the sun at noon, to illustrate all shadows, as the sheaves in harvest, to fill all penuries; all occasions invite His mercies, and all times are His seasons.[21]

---

[21] John Donne, Sermon preached in the evening of Christmas Day 1624, in *The Works of John Donne*, ed. H. Alford (London: Parker, 1839).

The worldview of the religious believer does not deny the 'benumbing' winter that so often afflicts the human spirit, but sees the divine nature as manifesting itself 'now', even in the midst of that winter darkness. The vision is of a God who becomes present in the world here and now, yet who somehow transcends it, bringing 'summer out of winter', yet in a way that goes beyond the normal seasonal processes of the natural world. Central to this theistic conception, then, is a strange dynamic tension between the presence or 'immanence' of God in the world, and God's 'transcendence', outreaching any boundaries of which we can conceive. To this tension between the 'here' and the 'beyond' we will now turn.

Chapter 2

The World 'Beyond'

Is that all there is?

Popular song[1]

1. The closing of the windows

In Philip Pullman's epic trilogy *His Dark Materials*, the young heroes, Will and Lyra, undertake a mysterious form of interdimensional travel, opening windows to other worlds or parallel universes. But at the end of the final volume they are told that all the windows must be closed:

> because if you thought that any still remained, you would spend your life searching for one, and that would be a waste of the time you have. You have other work than that to do, much more important and valuable, in your own world. There will be no travel outside it anymore.[2]

Reflecting on this in the final chapter, Lyra concludes that the Kingdom of Heaven is 'over': 'it is all finished. We shouldn't live as if it mattered more than this life in this world, because where we are is always the most important place.' The task instead is to 'be all those difficult things like cheerful and kind and curious

---

[1] Song by Jerry Leiber and Mike Stoller, recorded by Peggy Lee in 1969.
[2] Philip Pullman, *The Amber Spyglass* (London: Fickling, 2000), ch. 37.

and patient', and to study and work hard so that we can build ...
'Build what?', asks a sleepy voice. 'The Republic of Heaven',
answers Lyra.[3] And with that declaration, the book, and the
trilogy, ends.

Instead of worrying about a call beyond ourselves to some
'kingdom of heaven', Lyra decides to work towards something less
hierarchical, a *republic*, whose values and achievements depend
not on some higher power, but on how we ourselves, individually
and collectively, decide to act. The message is one that seems to
resonate with many people in our contemporary culture. The idea
that we should forget traditional religious tales of another better
world and get on with dealing with this one has a certain robust,
down-to-earth, appeal.

Yet on reflection there is something disquieting about
Pullman's conclusion; indeed, there is the hint of a tension, or
even a contradiction. For the trilogy has been a magnificent flight
of adventure, where the protagonists are constantly reaching
beyond themselves, and opening up new perspectives and new
realities. Can all this really end with a blank injunction to 'close
the windows'? Whatever Pullman may have intended this image
to convey, it's hard to see how human beings can ever rest content
with a 'closed' cosmos, one where they simply accept the conditions
and parameters determined by our biological nature and our social
structures, where we simply 'get on with it', stopping our ears to
any voice that seems to challenge us to reach beyond the confines
of our world as it is.

It is important to see that the puzzle confronting us here is
not about what people sometimes call the 'next world' or the
'after life'. I suggest we simply leave that question on one side
for the purposes of the present discussion. When Lyra decides

---

[3] Ibid.

to forget the 'Kingdom of Heaven' and work for a more down-to-earth 'Republic of Heaven', the issue at stake is not about whether there is a life after death. The question is about how we should spend our lives right now. And those readers who have followed Lyra's adventures up to this point know that she has spent her life up till now in a search, a mysterious and often dangerous journeying, a struggle with the forces of dark and light, a reaching out in hope and fear and trust towards the unknown. The 'subtle knife' that has enabled her and Will to open windows to 'other worlds' is what one might call an *instrument of transcendence* – it is a way of responding to that deepest of human impulses, to seek beyond the confines of the given. It is the impulse of which Alfred Tennyson spoke in his poem 'Ulysses', the impulse 'to strive, to seek, to find, and not to yield' – the impulse that makes the ageing hero refuse to lie down and rest after completing his long and arduous homeward journey to Ithaca, but to cry out instead:

> Come my friends
> 'Tis not too late to seek a newer world ...[4]

Ulysses will never give up the search to reach beyond himself. He will never abandon the quest for the 'transcendent', which we can take for present purposes to mean the idea of a domain of moral or spiritual significance that takes us *beyond* the ordinary routine world we inhabit. Transcendence is often contrasted with *immanence*, but the latter term is ambiguous. In theological usage it can mean the idea that the divine is present or manifest *in* the natural world, or even that everything there is is somehow an aspect of the divine ('in whom we live and

---

[4] Alfred Tennyson, 'Ulysses' (1833).

move and have our being', as St Paul's famous phrase has it).[5] But it can mean what we might call 'Radical Immanence' – the idea that all there is, and all that we can or should need in order to make the best of our lives, lies *here*, not elsewhere. Denying any transcendent dimension and accepting Radical Immanence is accepting that there is no ultimate meaning apart from what is to be found in *this* world, and in what we human agents choose to make of it.

'Radical Immanentism' is, in a way, the new orthodoxy of our times – a resolute 'closing of the windows', a proud insistence that we are self-sufficient, that we don't need transcendent aspirations, only our own human values. In the famous John Lennon song, we're told that it's easy, if we try, to 'imagine' there's no heaven.[6] We have a kind of hymn to Immanence, where above us is 'only sky', and below us only the earth, on which we humans must live as best we may. Here is the Oxford philosopher Adrian Moore expressing the same idea in a more sophisticated form, drawing on insights he finds in three successive thinkers from the seventeenth, nineteenth and twentieth centuries respectively: Baruch Spinoza, Friedrich Nietzsche and Gilles Deleuze:

> At the heart of what they most fundamentally share is a celebration of activity, an affirmation of life, in all its diversity. [They reject] the idea that life needs somehow to be justified, whether by some *telos* [goal] towards which everything is striving or by some transcendent structure in terms of which everything makes sense. Nature has no grand design. Nor is there anything transcendent to it. The celebration of

---

[5] Acts 17:28. Some theologians call this view 'panentheism'; see P. Clayton and A. Peacocke (eds), *In Whom We Live and Move and Have Our Being* (Grand Rapids, MI: Eerdmans, 2004).

[6] John Lennon, 'Imagine', 1971.

activity and the affirmation of life are the celebration and the affirmation of immanence.[7]

It sounds very upbeat. We would all like to celebrate and affirm life. But can we really do so wholeheartedly and with integrity within a framework of radical immanence? Are we really comfortable closing the windows on the transcendent?

There is a profound paradox here, one that goes to the heart of what it is to be human. Something like a framework of 'radical immanence' surrounds all the other animals with whom we share this planet. They work out their purposes responding to their innate biological drives and the stimuli from the world around them, attuned to the satisfaction of their needs, for food, for shelter, for reproduction. They are, in a sense, *stable systems*, even though over time the stress of changing conditions may of course favour particular mutations and cause some traits to die out and others to develop. As long as favourable circumstances obtain, they operate, as it were, within a 'closed' world, a world that they bump up against, exploit as best they may, but which they do not, and cannot, question. Human beings, by contrast, take nothing for granted. A surfeited, placid human, utterly content with its surroundings and in total equilibrium with them, would not be a true human, but simply a clever kind of animal. To be human is to be restless, to be troubled with a certain instability that drives us forward, reaching for more. And the paradox is that, however troubling we find this, something within us tells us that we cannot, we ought not, to wish it otherwise.

It is of course possible to get oneself into a frame of mind where one deplores this strange restlessness of our nature: we can start to suppose that we would be better off if we could simply 'close the windows' and settle down to deal with life as we find it. Milton

---

[7] Adrian Moore, *The Evolution of Modern Metaphysics: Making Sense of Things* (Cambridge: Cambridge University Press, 2012), pp. 248–9.

sometimes imagines the paradise of our primordial ancestors as depending on this kind of acceptance:

> Blest pair; and O yet happiest if ye seek
> No happier state, and *know to know no more*.[8]

And before his Fall, Adam seems to be of the same mind:

> to know
> That which before us lies in daily life,
> Is the prime Wisdom, what is more, is fume,
> Or emptiness, or fond impertinence,
> And renders us in things that most concerne
> Unpractis'd, unprepar'd, and still to seek.
> Therefore from this high pitch let us descend
> A lower flight, and speak of things at hand.[9]

And yet (and here comes the paradox once more), the very Adam who piously pronounces this mantra of humility has just been described by Milton as pondering eagerly on the mysteries of existence, the motions of the stars, and all manner of cosmic puzzles. The yearning to 'know more' will not go away. And Milton is of course fully aware of all the implications of this; for despite all his counselling of docile quiescence, the very nature of the human mind that he is portraying in Adam, the archetypal man, is a nature that cries out for the open-ended deployment of those extraordinary faculties that are unique to our species – faculties of rational inquiry, of speculation, of searching for truth.

The 'transcendent urges' we are talking about cannot be dismissed as idle curiosity, or as pointless aberrations, like the

---

[8]   John Milton, *Paradise Lost* [1674], Book IV, lines 774–5.
[9]   Ibid., Book VIII, lines 192–9.

urge to scratch an itch. They have always been considered to be signs of what is noblest in humanity, the unconquerable spirit that the ancient Greeks lauded in Prometheus, who aspired to reach the domain of the Gods. What is more, these impulses that mark out our true humanity are not merely concerned with intellectual inquiry. The 'reaching forward' is also a matter of deep emotional and imaginative sensibility, of moral yearnings, for self-improvement, for deeper awareness of the demands and mysteries of love and compassion, and also of 'aesthetic' yearnings (for want of a better term) – impulses to struggle upwards and attune ourselves to what is beautiful, not just passively but also actively, by creating shapes, words, colours and sounds that resonate with our sensibilities and give expressions to our longings.

All these characteristically human strivings are far more than just a matter of our pursuing regular patterns of useful activity. They are of a radically different order from the behaviour of a cow chomping the grass of the meadow, or a lion chasing a zebra, or even from normal human pursuits like those of the farmer tilling the fields or a weaver knitting clothes or a builder making a house to shelter a family. The 'transcendent' urges are quite different – they are signs of our determination to reach forward, past our weakness and our finitude, to what we are not yet, but might one day become. They take us beyond the 'immanent' world of useful toil and pleasant recreation, important and valuable though those things are, towards a world of value and meaning that is not obviously manifest in the material structures that compose our bodies and our environment, nor derived merely from our biologically and culturally inherited tastes and preferences, but which seems to reflect something richer, deeper and more awe-inspiring. Honesty and integrity demand that we find a way of acknowledging all this, and accommodating it somehow in our picture of the world. Religious ways of acknowledging it may not appeal to everyone, and as we all know there are many aspects of religion that are problematic, for all sorts of reasons. But for all their imperfections, and despite all the further questions they raise, the traditional frameworks of the great theistic religions do at least strive to find room for the transcendent, for that mysterious and ever-present dimension of our human existence that inspires us with awe and longing, and which we cannot deny while remaining true to our nature. Closing the windows is not an option.

2. Dimensions of reality

So far we have talked of various human strivings or longings that seem to carry us beyond the world of ordinary experience. But a sceptical critic may be inclined to ask how much work is really being done when we use this kind of spatial metaphor and talk of something *beyond* ordinary experience. Spatial talk often seems to crop up in this kind of context, and there are lots of variants on it: we may speak of something 'higher', something 'deeper', something 'outside' the normal – and indeed the word 'transcendent' is itself at root a spatial notion, implying a reality that goes beyond or *across* certain boundaries. And in explicitly religious terminology we find yet more variants on the spatial idea, for example the term 'supernatural', meaning literally 'above' or 'higher than' the natural.

Such metaphors may seem hard to cash out in any clearly intelligible way. Even the most ardent believer knows that heaven, or the transcendent realm, is not in any remotely literal sense 'up there' – 'above the bright blue sky', as the nineteenth-century children's hymn has it.[10] Faced with this, many people in our time have decided that it is best to abandon the idea of the transcendent altogether, and find some way of explaining away the longings in

---

[10] 'There's a friend for little children, above the bright blue sky' [1859], composed by the Sunday school teacher Albert Midlane.

more down-to-earth terms. An increasing number subscribe to the position philosophers know as 'naturalism' – the view that there is nothing beyond the natural world, or, more radically, that the very idea of a 'beyond' makes no sense. No doubt many readers of this book may have some inclination to identify with such a position, and may feel a sense of resistance when a theologian or a philosopher, or anyone else, tries to get them to believe in something called 'the supernatural'.

'Supernatural' is in any case a very unsatisfactory term, since it is a kind of blank, a placeholder (rather like 'non-material'). It purports to classify or inform, but actually it tells us little or nothing about the item so described. Clearly the God of traditional theism is conceived as having personal characteristics (such as compassion and faithfulness), so has to be thought of as a person, or as analogous to a person; but to add that he is a 'supernatural' person is unlikely to do much more for most people than to conjure up some vague and distinctly unhelpful notion of a Cartesian ghost or disembodied spirit. In any case, the term 'supernatural' implies a sharp antithesis between God and nature that is itself distinctly unsatisfactory. For 'nature' is a highly ambiguous term – one often used nowadays in a very restricted sense to refer to the empirical world as described by the language of science (hence the contemporary philosophical use of 'naturalism' to mean the view that nothing ultimately exists but this empirical world). But 'Nature', as used in medieval and early-modern philosophy – 'Nature' with a capital 'N', as it were – is the divinely created world, shot through with meaning and value. The existing cosmos is pervaded by the presence of God, the ultimate source of being, and in him, to repeat the Pauline phrase mentioned earlier, we of the natural world 'live and move and have our being'.[11] Indeed, the principal understanding of God, for

---

[11] Acts 17:28.

yes!.

the theist, is through nature, the wonders and beauties of which give us 'intimations of the transcendent'.[12] So nature is not just the blank, impersonal configuration of particles and forces described by modern physics, but comprises the magnificent whirling blaze of the galaxies, the wild rolling of the oceans, and the shimmering green of the woods in spring. The world, the natural world, is, for the theist 'charged with the grandeur of God', as Gerard Manley Hopkins put it. To label God as 'supernatural' is thus to risk removing him from the very manifestation of the sacred here in the natural world, which is one of our most important modes of access to the divine.[13]

But is such talk of the 'divine' as manifest in the natural world justified in the first place? If we think of the reactions of awe and wonder just mentioned, or of the 'transcendent' strivings discussed in the previous section, our longings to reach beyond our finitude, let it be granted that these are things which spring from deep within our human nature. But does admitting this require a religious worldview? Isn't it possible to acknowledge our 'spiritual' longings while at the same time resisting a religious interpretation? Rather belatedly, the so-called 'new atheists' or 'militant atheists' have begun to realize that they might have done better in their propaganda war if they paid more attention to these deep human impulses. Christopher Hitchens, towards the end of his life, declared in a debate:

> I'm a materialist ... yet there is something beyond the material, or not entirely consistent with it, what you could call the Numinous, the Transcendent ... It's in certain music,

---

[12] See John Cottingham, *Philosophy of Religion: Towards a More Humane Approach* (Cambridge: Cambridge University Press, 2014), ch. 3, section 4.

[13] For more on the terms 'natural', 'supernatural' and 'naturalism', see Fiona Ellis, *God, Value, and Nature* (Oxford: Oxford University Press, 2014).

landscape, certain creative work, and without this we really would merely be primates. It's important to appreciate … that, and religion has done a very good job of enshrining it in music and architecture.[14]

Similarly, Sam Harris, another prominent spokesman for the new atheism, has observed that

spiritual experiences often constitute the most important and transformative moments in a person's life. Not recognizing that such experiences are possible or important can make us appear less wise even than our craziest religious opponents.[15]

So the suggestion is that so-called 'transcendent' aspirations and experiences are available to the non-believer as well as the believer. On this view, the 'spiritual' dimension of experience, the dimension of the 'sacred' as it has often been called in religious parlance, does not in fact require religious belief at all, but simply arises from certain kind of special sensitivity to the purely natural world we live in.

It can't be denied that experiences of the 'numinous', as Hitchens calls it, for example experiences of awe and wonder at the beauty of nature and great art, can come to everyone irrespective of religious allegiance or its lack. I would say they are part of our human birthright, not frequent or everyday, but nevertheless universal, in the sense that they are available in principle to everyone,

---

[14] Christopher Hitchens, in debate with Tony Blair [2010], quoted in Jules Evans, 'The New Atheists are actually transcendentalists', http://philosophyforlife. org/the-new-atheists-are-actually-transcendentalists, posted 24 January 2014 (accessed 17 April 2015).

[15] 'The Problem with Atheism', *The Washington Post*, October 2, 2007, cited in Evans, 'The New Atheists' (see previous note).

sometimes even despite the gravest distress or oppression. But the interesting question is not whether you have to be a believer to have such experiences – clearly you do not – but rather whether such experiences can be properly accommodated, or made sense of, in terms of a purely secular worldview.

For the hard-nosed materialist–atheist, describing such experiences as 'transcendent', 'numinous' or 'sacred' will be simply a *façon de parler* – a way of talking that lacks any ontological basis, or, in other words, which does not point to any ultimate objective reality. On this view, the natural world studied by science is, ontologically speaking, all that there really is; though there may be heightened or altered states of consciousness, like those Sam Harris has expressed an interest in studying (produced, he says, by fasting, meditation and 'psychotropic plants'),[16] these are understood as purely subjective effects of various brain changes, arising as by-products of evolved physiological processes originally generated by the needs of survival in the ordinary natural world. The idea of anything more to the story than this, anything ontologically extra that transcends the material world, is for Harris and those who think like him simply an illusion, resulting from the fact that we humans are 'deeply disposed to broadcast our own subjectivity onto the world',[17] or, as the Scottish atheist philosopher David Hume put it long ago in the eighteenth century, 'the mind has a great propensity to spread itself on external objects'.[18]

The underlying worldview here is one that has had a tight hold on the imagination of a large number of philosophers ever since the seventeenth century. It is a picture according to which the real world 'out there' is the world studied by natural science, the world

---

[16] Sam Harris, *The End of Faith* (New York: Norton, 2005), ch. 7, p. 210.

[17] Sam Harris, 'The Mortal Dangers of Religious Faith', interview at http://www.amazon.com/gp/feature.html?docId=542154 (accessed 17 April 2015).

[18] David Hume, *A Treatise of Human Nature* [1739–40], Book I, part III, section xiv.

of particle interactions, of atoms and molecules, of mass and energy, of all that can be represented in the quantitative language of mathematical physics, or which is made up of components that can be so represented. Biological beings, plants, animals and human beings are an accepted part of reality on this picture, but their status as genuine entities with objective existence depends on the fact that they are made up of cells, which are in turn made up of molecules or atoms or whatever can be described in the language of physics. But the human world of value and meaning, on this physicalist picture, has an altogether more shadowy and more secondary kind of existence: it is a kind of temporary effluent or by-product of our human brains. What is *really* happening, happening at the hard-core ultimate level of reality, is the various physical events and processes comprising the external environment in which we live, together with the neurological events going on in the cerebral cortices of the species *homo sapiens*. And these neurological events are in turn determined by the way the external physical events impinge on our nervous systems, together with the genetically determined structures in our brains which organize and process the resulting causal inputs.

Notice that this picture makes no room for anything 'transcendent'. The particle interactions out there in the environment, plus the particle interactions inside our brains – this is all there really is. It is conceded by the materialist (as in the passages from the atheist writers quoted above) that the experiences corresponding to some of our brain states may be very important in our lives, and that we may be profoundly stirred by some moral emotion, such as compassion, or some aesthetic feeling, as when we watch a beautiful sunset; but neither of these, nor indeed any other aspect of our experience in which we seem to reach out beyond ourselves to a richer and more resonant reality – none of this can for them have any objective foundation. For on the picture we are discussing there is nothing for it to correspond to, no really existing domain of the numinous or the sacred, just the continuous unfolding of particle interactions and neurological processing.

But once we start to reflect on this kind of picture there is something very odd about it. Why should this privilege be accorded to the world of physical particle interactions – the privilege of being more 'real', more 'ultimate' than anything else? A moment's reflection shows us that even if physical science is taken as the ultimate measure of reality, very large entities, such as stars and planetary systems and galaxies, must be allowed to be just as 'real', just as genuine, and just as legitimate objects of scientific study as molecules and atoms. But if stars and planets are real (and what scientist could deny it?), then clearly mountains and hills and valleys and flowers and streams and meadows are just as real. And if the latter objects are real, are not the various *features* of those objects, the vivid greenness of the meadows, the shimmering beauty of the flowers, the majestic sweep of the hills and valleys, also real?

At this point, however, those who take the materialist or reductionist line under discussion will dig in their heels. Yes, galaxies and planets and mountains are real enough, as real as the atoms and molecules that compose them; so much can be granted. And certainly they have genuine measurable properties that impinge on us and affect us in various ways, through our sensory organs and nervous systems. But it's very different, so it will be objected, when we apply terms like 'beautiful' or 'majestic' to the flowers or the mountains: for then, it will be claimed, we are no longer referring to anything real, but are simply projecting our own subjective reactions onto the world. So once again (so runs the argument) there is no room for anything 'sacred' or 'numinous' or 'transcendent' – or at least not in a way that allows any supposed reality outside the scope of the physical sciences; there are only the objects studied by the various sciences (the mountains, the rivers, the grass, and the underlying particles and forces), and then the quirky subjective reactions of human beings who mistakenly proceed to 'spread' their own responses on to external reality. And even these quirky subjective responses, so it is argued, will one day be explained by science, once we understand more about how the brain works. Once all these scientific explanations are finally in place, there will be no room whatever for the transcendent, because there will be nothing, literally nothing, that transcends or outruns the scope of science.

3. Science, scientism and subjectivity

I want to maintain that there *is* room for a genuine transcendent reality, and hence that the world picture just sketched is profoundly mistaken. But it's vital to see that in so arguing I am not in any way disparaging science, or denying its achievements. It is a deplorable fact that in the past so many defenders of religion have presumed to take issue with the findings of science; one thinks of the resistance in the seventeenth century to the discoveries of Galileo about the sun-centred planetary system, or in the nineteenth century (with some diehards persisting even to this day) the opposition to the Darwinian theory of natural selection. Of course, no scientific theory is the final truth, and (as any good scientist will admit) no theory can be accepted dogmatically as the last word. But nevertheless, the hard-won methods of science – careful observation, controlled experiment, mathematical modelling – have proved to be wonderfully successful tools for uncovering the workings of the universe, and the resulting discoveries are among the greatest achievements of humankind. Truth is indivisible: no genuine truth can conflict with any other truth; so if there *are* truths of religion, for example about a transcendent reality, those truths must necessarily be compatible with any of the truths discovered by science. The religious believer thus has no business taking issue with the genuine discoveries of science, but on the contrary should warmly welcome them as illuminating and enriching our understanding of reality as a whole.

This last point is particularly relevant to the scientific work on the human brain that has gathered pace in our own times. There is now overwhelming evidence that all our human cognitive and emotional and appetitive and sensory faculties depend for their operation on the workings of the brain; once again, there should be no need for the defender of a religious worldview to deny that fact, or to try to maintain that the human mind operates as a ghostly immaterial entity somehow 'lodged' in the machine of the body, as the philosopher René Descartes is popularly supposed to have maintained.[19]

So having conceded that much, how can one still maintain that there is room for a 'transcendent' dimension – a dimension that outruns the reach of science? If the truths of science are accepted, and indeed enthusiastically affirmed, don't we have to accept that science is the last word on the ultimate nature of reality? It depends on what you mean by 'the last word'. If what is meant is that any claim about ultimate reality must be *compatible* with the true discoveries of science, this is clearly right: there is no future for a religious or any other outlook that tries to contradict or set aside the findings of science. But if what is meant is that *scientific truth comprises all the truth there is*, that is a very different matter. The claim that there is no truth outside of science is not itself a piece of science; how could it be, for what scientific procedures could possibly establish it? It is not science, but *scientism* – the

---

[19] See René Descartes, *Meditations* [*Meditationes de prima philosophia*, 1641], Sixth Meditation. Descartes' full account of the human mind is however far more complex and more nuanced than the theory nowadays known – and scathingly dismissed – as 'Cartesian dualism'; see John Cottingham, *Cartesian Reflections* (Oxford: Oxford University Press, 2008), chs 1 and 9.

unargued assertion that there is no ultimate truth or reality except what is disclosed by using the methods and descriptions of science.

To say the scope of science comprises all reality is not only an unargued assertion – it is patently false. To see just one reason why it is false, consider a very familiar sort of scenario: two people sitting at a table conversing. You, the person now sitting opposite me across the table, are real – as real as anything in the universe. Yet you are in a certain sense *inaccessible* to me (the observer), and therefore to science. What do I mean by 'inaccessible'? Clearly, I can see you, can look into your eyes, can converse with you. I know perfectly well that you have thoughts and feelings just as I do (so forget that tiresome philosophical puzzle known as the 'problem of other minds'). Nevertheless, there is a whole world, *your world*, the world that is vividly present to you as a subject, which I can never enter. I can move to your side of the table, and even ask to sit in the chair you were occupying so I can see how the room looks from that side, but this gets me no closer to your world. It merely adds something to mine. I can never enter fully into your perspective, the world that is unique to you, your 'lifeworld', or *Lebenswelt*, to use the German term: the world of which you are the subject and the centre.

Science cannot unlock this door. Study your brain waves as I will, measure the firing of the neurons in your brain, analyse the chemical reactions that take place there … none of this can ever enable me to enter your 'lifeworld'. Suppose, said the early-modern philosopher Gottfried Leibniz, that the brain was blown up to the size of a factory or a mill (*moulin*), so that we could enter and look around. What would we see? Merely parts that interact with one another, he answered, not the meaningful world of perceptions and thoughts and feelings that makes up your conscious life.[20] Science,

---

[20] Gottfried Leibniz, *Monadology* [*La Monadologie*, 1714], §17.

by its very nature, dissects and analyses *objects* or *events*, and it does so very well. But it cannot encompass *subjects*. As the scientific observer sits across the table from you, she can never reach your inmost self, the self that is the conscious centre of all the experiences you are having.

It is easy to misunderstand the notion of a lifeworld. Nothing said so far should be taken to imply that each of us is hermetically sealed within a wholly subjective domain. Edmund Husserl, who coined the idea of a personal 'lifeworld' (*Lebenswelt*), stressed that each person's individual consciousness operates through a nexus of meanings that depend on an intersubjective context of shared language.[21] Similarly, the great twentieth-century philosophical genius Ludwig Wittgenstein stressed the importance of language, community and interpersonal behaviour when it comes to understanding the mind and its contents, and famously criticized the conception of a 'private' inner world of the mind.[22] Later philosophers have followed this lead. 'Meanings', the American philosopher Hilary Putnam trenchantly observed, 'ain't in the head'.[23] To understand the meaning of what someone is thinking about, we need to refer *outwards*, to the complex social network of human interaction that generates all our conceptual resources and allows us to describe and interpret our experience.

Nevertheless, even when all this is taken into account, there remains something unique about your lifeworld, something that depends on your own special personal history and individual perspective. So suppose we take on board all the Wittgensteinian

---

[21] See Edmund Husserl, *Cartesian Meditations* [*Cartesianische Meditationen*, 1931], trans. D. Cairns (The Hague: Nijhoff, 1960), §§57ff.

[22] Ludwig Wittgenstein, *Philosophical Investigations* [*Philosophische Untersuchungen*, 1953], trans. G. E. M. Anscombe (New York: Macmillan, 1958), §§243–315.

[23] Hilary Putnam, 'The Meaning of Meaning' [1975], in *Philosophical Papers*, vol. 2 (Cambridge: Cambridge University Press, 1985).

lessons of the previous paragraph, as we should: suppose we accept that understanding the nature of the human mind requires us to look outwards to culture and the rules of language, and also to our bodily behaviour as we interact with other human beings. And suppose we also take on board all the results of neuroscience as it investigates the workings of our brains, which enable us to respond to this wider world in all the rich and complex ways that human beings do. Suppose, in short, that as I am sitting across the table from you I have at my disposal a complete description of your behaviour, a complete history of your upbringing, your induction into a linguistic community, and all your subsequent interactions with everyone you have met. And suppose further that I have a complete printout of the entire complicated sequence of brain activity, without which none of the relevant behaviour and social interaction could have been possible. Even with all this at my disposal, the unique lifeworld that belongs to you as the subject of all this experience will still remain inaccessible to me.

There is nothing 'spooky' or *contra-scientific* about this, though it is *extra-scientific* – outside the scope of science. The reason I cannot reach you as a subject is not that you are some ghostly, immaterial being whose operations cannot be detected. All that you do and are is intimately dependent on your biological nature and your brain workings, and these can of course be studied by science, along with all your behaviour and your interactions with others. But for all that, your lifeworld, the way the world presents itself to you as a conscious subject, remains beyond my reach, just as my lifeworld does for you. The issue here is not a scientific one, but is rather (to use a problematic term) a metaphysical one. It concerns our status as *subjects*, and subjects are as real as anything could be, and yet in some fundamental way beyond the observable realities investigated by science. Human beings can of course be measured and weighed, and all our inner physiological workings investigated, but as subjects we are ultimately shielded from the gaze of others. Even two lovers, however intimately joined, even when they spend their lives together and understand each other as closely as is possible for two human beings, will still be unable to enter into each other's lifeworlds.

4. Transcendence and presence

The strange *inaccessibility of the subject* that we have just been exploring may be an interesting phenomenon, but it might not seem to take us any further towards the religious idea of a transcendent reality. On the contrary, it might at first seem to be merely a rather gloomy and unavoidable feature of human life, generating a kind of 'metaphysical loneliness', as Roger Scruton has termed it: I can never fully reach you in your being as a subject of experience like myself.[24] Yet, as we have seen, reflecting on the unique 'lifeworld' that each of us enjoys as a subject does at least show how much of reality lies beyond the scope of scientific description.

It is often said that we live in a disenchanted world, meaning (in part) that modern science has dispelled the crude animistic idea of a world haunted by mysterious spirits and other occult powers. That may be true. But there is more than one kind of enchantment. The triumphs of modern science in explaining and predicting the course of nature do nothing to dispel the vividness and the wonder of the lifeworld to which each human subject has direct access. There is something almost miraculous, and certainly very wonderful, about the way in which the world is so vividly and directly present to each of us. As I raise my eyes, there before me is the grass, shimmering and green, the trees rustling in the breeze, the white clouds racing across the sky, the whole world, given to me like a gift, present to my gaze, directly accessible, a world in which I can move and breathe and live, and which is in

---

[24] Roger Scruton, *The Face of God* (London: Continuum, 2012), p. 155.

a certain sense *my* world. And for you it is the same: you have your own unique lifeworld that is vividly present to you and distinct from mine (even though our worlds are related and interconnected through networks of interpersonal meaning and language). And all this is as real as can be, not a mere shadow or by-product or 'epiphenomenon', but the very touchstone of truth: anyone who denies it, or tells us that some other world (of mathematical entities, or particle interactions, or spirits, or anything else) is 'more real' than the lifeworld of which I and you have immediate awareness, is denying the fundamentally *present* reality that has to be the basis on which any philosophical or scientific theorizing must ultimately be built.

This is a reality that we might call 'transcendent', if only in the limited sense that it outruns, or eludes, the capacity of science to analyse and objectify it. But I think it may also provide the first step for pointing us towards transcendent reality in the much deeper and richer sense that is the object of the religious quest. To see this, let us reflect further about the reality, the 'being', if you will, that is disclosed in the 'lifeworld' of each of us – the rich tapestry of being that presents itself to you and me as experiencing subjects. For each of us, this reality, this tapestry of being, is 'my world', the world present to me as a subject. But if it is 'my' world, then what happens when I cease to be? My lifeworld will be no more, though of course yours will continue if you survive me. But what happens when the last human being expires? Atoms will still collide and fuse, energy exchanges will still continue, but will the world now be, as it were, a blank, a world where there will be no more 'presence'? Here is the American philosopher Mark Johnston pondering on this theme:

> On the standard view of the relation between consciousness and reality, most of being is absolutely wasted, for only an infinitesimally small fraction of what exists is ever *present*,

that is, ever discloses or reveals some aspect of its nature. On this view, when the last individual consciousness ceases to be, the very local phenomenon of *presence* will end. The lights will have gone out, all over the universe, never to go on again.[25]

It is very hard, though, to get our minds round this idea of a 'dark' or 'blank' world, a world where nothing is 'present'. Part of what is odd about such a picture is that it seems to make the 'presence' of the world depend on *us* (or creatures likes us). By assuming that the 'lights will go out' after the expiry of the last individual's lifeworld, it implicitly treats us conscious subjects as *producers of presence* – that is, beings whose thoughts and feelings are the very preconditions of presence or disclosure. Without us human beings (or some other conscious creatures elsewhere in the universe) there would, on the picture we are now considering, *be* no presence. The whole of being would be, as it were, *wasted*, since there would be no one to make it present through their conscious thinking and sensing.

In a theistic worldview, by contrast, where there is a transcendent personal consciousness at the heart of reality, 'presence' is no longer produced merely by me or you; it is no longer dependent on the puny flickering of your or my consciousness. Instead of the strange, blank, picture of reality as 'wasted' once the 'lights go out' and the last conscious subject expires, now instead we have a picture of the world, as long as it endures, as always remaining *present*, objectively *there*, held in being by the universal sustaining mind of God.

---

[25] Mark Johnston, *Saving God: Religion after Idolatry* (Princeton, NJ: Princeton University Press, 2009), p. 131; emphasis supplied. My citing of Johnston's illuminating work does not imply acceptance of his (often highly idiosyncratic) proposals for reconfiguring religious belief within a naturalistic framework.

Many contemporary philosophers have found themselves unable to accept this theistically grounded picture of how reality is 'present', but it is interesting to see how non-theistic thinkers like Mark Johnston seem implicitly drawn to it, almost in spite of their official professions of atheism. Johnston, in the passage referred to above, goes on to suggest that we should stop thinking of ourselves as 'producers of presence', and think of ourselves instead as mere *samplers of presence*. The vivid lifeworld of which each of us is the subject is not after all a matter of our *making* things present through our thoughts and sensations, argues Johnston, but rather is a matter of our *sampling* a small and highly selective part of the universal Being or reality which, as it were, broadcasts itself far and wide. On this hypothesis, as Johnston puts it, 'Being is *by its nature present*.' Or again, 'Being's fundamental activity is *self-disclosure*.'[26]

The outlook Johnston proceeds to develop from these ideas is certainly not a traditional theistic one, since he resolutely rejects the idea of a God who has any direct interest in his creatures, or seeks their good. But his using the term 'Being' with a capital 'B' is nevertheless significant, calling to mind the usage of Martin Heidegger, which is often interpreted as a way of referring to what people mean by 'God'. At all events, what Johnston means by 'Being' is a supreme reality that *makes itself present* to us finite beings: 'the general form of reality is … the outpouring of Being itself … and its self-disclosure'.[27] And what follows from this, according to Johnston, speaking now in a tone highly reminiscent of religious language, is that we should feel a 'profound background feeling of gratitude in response to the "doubly donatary" character of reality'.[28] There is a twofold

---

[26] Johnston, *Saving God*, p. 132.
[27] *Saving God*, p. 156.
[28] *Saving God*, p. 156.

gift, firstly the basic gift whereby (like each of us) I am, just in virtue of existing, an expression of Being, albeit a finite and limited example. I am, as it were, caught up in the total mystery of Being, just in virtue of being here, and being alive: 'the force that through the green fuse drives the flower drives my green life'.[29] But, secondly, there is the further gift whereby all of this, the reality that is my lifeworld, is present to me, or, as Johnston puts it, 'made available to me, gratis'.[30]

For the religious believer who interprets all this in terms of a theistic worldview, such feelings of joy and gratitude are taken much further than Johnston takes them. As we have seen, Johnston helps himself to religious language like 'gift' (or 'donation') and gratitude; but by the end of his account he pulls back and tries to reduce the feeling to one of mere amazement at the remarkable fact that, in a purely naturalistic universe, I should happen to exist, and to have conscious awareness: 'Whatever happens … I have already won the cosmic lottery.' But for the believer, by contrast, over and above such amazement there is a feeling of mystery and awe at the gift of 'presence'; there is, in addition, a realization that the gift of presence and the spontaneous upwelling of gratitude implies the presence of a *giver*. The naturalist may try to fudge this and simply say we are lucky to be here, and that the chances against our existing are huge, so we ought to be pleased. But gratitude is something different, something more: it is a *personal* emotion, directed to the bestower of the gift. Or, as a hymn of praise by the poet Robert Bridges puts it,

> Daily doth the almighty giver
> Bounteous gifts on us bestow;
> His desire our soul delighteth

---

[29] First line of a poem by Dylan Thomas, published in *18 Poems* [1943], quoted in Johnston, *Saving God*, p. 157.

[30] *Saving God*, p. 157.

Pleasure leads us where we go.
Love doth stand
At his hand;
Joy doth wait at his command.[31]

Support or justification for these much richer expressions of love and gratitude must await further argument. But let us conclude the present chapter with some final reflections on transcendence and on the idea of 'gift'.

An ancient image of the world given as a *gift* to humankind is found in the familiar story of the garden of Eden, the paradise given by God to our primordial ancestors (or, if you prefer, to the archetypal or symbolic representatives of humankind). But calling the original paradise a 'garden' may be much more than a casual metaphor. As the British philosopher David Cooper has pointed out, the concept of a garden implies a kind of unity, or 'intimate co-dependence' between human beings and the natural world. Putting it this way already carries a certain spiritual or quasi-religious resonance, if only because traditional religious virtues (such as discipline, humility and hope) are needed in bringing that co-dependence to fruition, in flower and harvest. This makes it appropriate to call gardening a kind of spiritual activity, which can contribute to, and be partly constitutive of, human flourishing. Yet beyond such co-dependence between human endeavour and the natural world, Cooper argues that the garden can also be thought of as an 'epiphany of man's relationship to mystery': the co-dependence between man and nature 'itself embodies or refers us to the co-dependence of human existence and the "deep ground" of the world and ourselves'.[32]

---

[31] From the hymn 'All My Hope on God is Founded' by Robert Bridges, in *The Yattendon Hymnal*, 1899, (based on the seventeenth-century German hymn *Meiner Hoffnung stehet feste*).

[32] David Cooper, *A Philosophy of Gardens* (Oxford: Clarendon Press, 2006), p. 145.

In explaining this revelation of co-dependence, Cooper refers to an evocative portrait by the painter Paul Cézanne of his gardener Vallier, sitting tranquilly amid the foliage.[33] Cézanne himself once described nature as a 'catechism' by the author of nature, a 'show spread before us by *Pater Omnipotens ... Deus* [God the Almighty Father]'. The idea of reality as given, or spread out before us, calls to mind Johnston's idea of 'donation', or the 'outpouring of Being'; but once again, like Johnston, Cooper insists that the deeper sense of world's, or the garden's, meaning need not take a specifically theistic form. He proposes as an alternative the Zen Buddhist conception that speaks of gardens as embodying a 'presence of transcendence' that 'infuses human activity with a sense of governing spiritual purposes'.[34] The old gardener in Cezanne's portrait is 'thoughtfully serene' (*gelassen*), as Martin Heidegger put it in his own poetic reflection on the painting in question.[35] The gardener is 'attentively listening', in the words of the ancient Japanese garden treatise, the *Sakuteiki*, to the 'request made by the earth'.[36]

Among the rich cluster of interlinked notions that have emerged from our brief excursion into the arguments of Cooper and of Johnston are those of 'presence', 'gift', 'transcendence', 'attention' and 'letting be', all of which are in a certain sense religious notions, albeit deployed by philosophers who explicitly repudiate a theistic framework for interpreting them. But whether the theistic framework can be dispensed with as easily as they suppose is far from clear. When Cooper, for example, interprets 'letting be' as 'allowing things to be experienced as the "gifts" they are',[37]

---

[33] Paul Cézanne, 'Le Jardinier Vallier' [*c*.1906], http://www.tate.org.uk/art/artworks/cezanne-the-gardener-vallier-n04724 (accessed 15 April 2015).

[34] Cooper, *A Philosophy of Gardens*, p. 144.

[35] Martin Heidegger, 'Cézanne' (1970).

[36] Cooper, *A Philosophy of Gardens*, p. 158.

[37] *A Philosophy of Gardens*, p. 158.

it seems that, like Johnston with his 'double donation',[38] he may be taking an unauthorized loan from the theistic capital that he officially repudiates. True thankfulness has no really secure place in a worldview where 'gift' is nothing but a specious metaphor.[39] Or again, it is difficult to see how a Buddhist view of the cosmos, which regards it as ultimately no more than an impersonal and transient flux, is entitled to help itself to teleological notions like that of 'governing spiritual purposes'.

Such reservations notwithstanding, both the philosophers we have been discussing seem to me to show an admirable sensitivity, all too rare in our contemporary anglophone philosophical climate, to what might be called *the depth and mystery of being*. Like many writers wrestling with the loss of traditional religious faith, their work manifests an understandable desire to find a worldview that respects the immeasurable riches of science and the scientific way of thinking, but resists its takeover by science's arrogant and degenerate cousin, scientism.[40] The struggle to take seriously such notions as 'presence' and 'gift' is part of the struggle to find an outlook that does justice to the true richness and wonder of our human experience of the world. And as we have seen, the first step here is to acknowledge the irreducibly personal dimension of reality, manifest in our access to the lifeworld that is present to each of us, like a gift. And the next step is to acknowledge that gift as grounded in a reality that freely bestows itself on each of us.

But reaching this level of insight immediately propels us a step further. For the reality to which we have access, that which we are given, is not merely 'there', like a gift lying on the table, nor is it just 'provided' as a commodity to be used at whim. What we seem to glimpse, in many of our experiences of what is given, is

---

[38] Johnston, *Saving God*, p. 156.

[39] But see Michael Lacewing, 'Can non-theists appropriately feel existential gratitude?', *Religious Studies*, 2015.

[40] For the distinction between science and scientism, see the previous section.

something that calls to us and demands a *response*, beckoning us onwards to transcend ourselves. The word 'glimpse' is important here. We are not dealing with impersonally accessible scientific evidence, but with what, for the theistic believer, is a kind of *sign* – a sign that I can only respond to by reaching in awe and love towards the transcendent power that is the source of the gift. What is glimpsed, moreover, is not something that concerns only myself, for in recognizing the gift that is made present to me as a finite conscious subject, I cannot but grasp that each of us, each finite conscious subject, is also a receiver. I have no more right to this gift than anyone else; we are all dependent, all undeserving receivers of the mystery of being. And in recognizing this, I also somehow glimpse that the call to transcend myself and reach out in awe and love towards the source of the gift is also a call to reach out in love and respect to each finite created subject, for the mystery embraces them too. But this is to anticipate further vital steps in the journey towards belief, which remain to be explored.

Chapter 3

Adopting a Worldview

Ein Bild hielt uns gefangen. ['A picture held us captive.']

Ludwig Wittgenstein[1]

1. Outlooks, pictures, frameworks, lenses

There are no doubt many different ways of coming to believe something. The most common is an almost instantaneous process, as when you believe there is a chair in the corner of the room, or that your cup of coffee has gone cold. Such ordinary basic beliefs are formed pretty much involuntarily, when you look round the room, or take a sip of coffee. In this kind of belief-formation process, the mind seems almost passive: the data from the senses are processed by the brain, and the belief spontaneously forms itself in the mind, 'just like that'. There is the chair; the coffee is cold. End of story.

Very different from this is the case where there is a more active contribution from the agent, as when someone examines the evidence for a proposition before reaching a decision on what to believe. For example, she sees spots of water on the window pane, opens the window and holds her hand out, and, after a moment or two's waiting, decides that the rain has now stopped.

---

[1] Ludwig Wittgenstein, *Philosophical Investigations* [*Philosophische Untersuchungen*, 1953], trans. G. E. M. Anscombe (New York: Macmillan, 1958), §115.

Both these ways of believing are familiar enough, and conceivably a person might come to religious belief in one of these two relatively straightforward ways, or something analogous to them. But I suspect that what characteristically and typically turns someone into a religious believer is an altogether different kind of process, more radical in terms of the psychological changes undergone, and more comprehensive and all-pervasive in its scope and extent.

We have spoken in the previous chapters of contrasting 'visions' of the world, and touched on notions such as that of a 'worldview' or a 'picture of reality'. In the German language, always more comfortable with compound nouns than English, it is common to speak of an individual or a society having a *Weltanschauung*, literally a 'world-outlook'. The German term has had a variety of meanings since it was first coined (albeit in a rather special sense) in the late eighteenth century,[2] but has been widely adopted into English as an accepted way of referring to a general system of ideas or a comprehensive system of thought.

Although a system of thought is a complicated structure which may have many ramifications, it can often have at its centre a certain simple and vivid picture of the way things are. Sometimes such a picture may take hold of us almost without our being aware of it, as Ludwig Wittgenstein points out in our opening epigraph for this chapter, where the context is how the structure of language can predispose us to think in a certain way, and indeed mislead us, or 'bewitch the intelligence', as he puts it elsewhere.[3] But other pictures may be more benign, as when Wittgenstein speaks of a religious outlook as involving the feeling of absolute safety: 'nothing can injure me, whatever happens'. This sort of attitude,

---

[2]   By Immanuel Kant, *Critique of Judgement* [*Kritik der Urteilskraft*, 1790], Part I, book 2, §26.

[3]   Wittgenstein, *Philosophical Investigations*, §109.

Wittgenstein went on to say, is obviously different from a feeling of safety about some ordinary matter, such as feeling secure that you can't get whooping cough because you've had it once already. To ordinary, common-sense ways of thinking, you might well be safe from whooping cough, but there are obviously other diseases you could get, so to say you are safe 'whatever happens' is, in a literal sense, nonsense. But this should not lead us to dismiss such language out of hand, since it is inevitable that thinking about religion will sooner or later 'run up against the boundaries of language'. Such thinking, according to Wittgenstein, springs from a tendency in the human mind that demands 'deep respect', even though it might not add to our factual knowledge.[4]

Despite such expressions of sympathy for religious ways of thinking, Wittgenstein was himself unable to embrace any traditional religious world picture, although he continued to wrestle with what was involved in adopting a religious outlook. In one of the places where he discusses religious belief, he speaks of it as involving commitment 'to a set of co-ordinates' (*zu einem Koordinatensystem*). A variant reading has the more general phrase 'a system of reference' (*einem Bezugssystem*).[5] One of the thoughts underlying this comparison may be that a system of reference, or a system of measurement (for example the metric system), is something that is adopted even though it cannot itself be verified in the way that a given measurement within the system ('this stick is three metres long') can be verified. The metric system does not itself belong in the complete set of true propositions expressing metric measurements; rather, it is a *framework* that generates the possibility of such measurements. So Wittgenstein may be

[4] Ludwig Wittgenstein, 'A Lecture on Ethics' [1929], in *Philosophical Review* (January 1965), pp. 3–12, at p. 8.
[5] Ludwig Wittgenstein, manuscript of 1947, in *Culture and Value*, ed. Georg Henrik Wright, Heikki Nyman and Alois Pichler (Oxford: Blackwell, 1998), p. 73.

suggesting that a religious outlook does not refer to objects or items within the world but instead provides a general framework for understanding and interpreting it.

But not all frameworks are equally congenial to everyone. If we pursue the metric analogy, it is clear that there are some anti-Europeans in early twenty-first-century Great Britain who deplore the adoption of the metric system, and greatly prefer more 'human' measurements like the foot and the yard, originally based on traditional ways of pacing out distances. Whether or not we sympathize with this, there is no contradiction, in this type of debate, in someone saying 'You stick to your system and I'll stick to mine.' Neither system is 'the right one' in any fundamental sense, nor are they really in conflict (though of course people may be anxious for political or cultural reasons to champion one over the other).

What is at stake in the measurement example is thus not truth, but convenience or utility or pleasingness, or something of that sort. But in the religious case, when people give their allegiance to a given framework or picture of reality such as theism, they do so because they believe it to be *true*. Perhaps, in so far as it may shape our thoughts and actions, it can be compared to a 'system of co-ordinates', but for the believer this is not just a matter of convenience or personal preference. It is taken by the believer to be a system that genuinely reflects the structure of reality, uncovers the true purpose and meaning of human existence, and serves as a valid and trustworthy guide to how we should live our lives. And this in turn raises the question of how we can decide whether the theistic picture of reality is true. How can we know whether to accept the idea of a personal God and put it at the centre of our outlook on the world?

The religious sceptic will already have answered this last question by saying we *can't* know, and will go on to say that in the absence of any compelling evidence there can be no reason to consider accepting it. One has to admit that there is a certain robust reasonableness about this, calling to mind the definition of a sceptic (best uttered in a dry and cautious tone) as 'one who prefers his statements to be true'. The guiding principle at work here is what one might call an *epistemology of detachment*. If we dramatize the process of assessing a picture of reality and imagine the religious worldview as a picture in the literal sense, like a painting hung in a gallery, the sceptic can be thought of as one who stands back, detached and critical, cautiously scrutinizes the object from a distance, raises a doubtful eyebrow, shakes his head and calmly walks on.

The simile does not quite work, however. For if, as suggested a moment ago, a worldview functions as a 'framework of interpretation', then it will hardly be comparable to a particular painting, hung in a gallery alongside others. On reflection, it is clear that a framework of interpretation could not be the kind of thing that can be assessed in the way a single item in a collection can be assessed, since it is not an 'item' or 'object' at all. If we have to find a simile for the kind of thing it is, we might say it is more like a *lens*: not an item in the collection, but that which enables us to see the collection in the first place, or to bring it into proper focus so as to grasp its significance.

Unfortunately, though, the 'lens' model is not quite satisfactory either, or at least it raises further difficulties of its own. Taken one way, it might suggest an implanted lens in the eye, like a pair of spectacles that it is impossible to take off. One thinks here of the philosopher Immanuel Kant's theory that our human experience of the world is necessarily structured in terms of notions like space and time and causality, so that we cannot but process the world around us in these terms, and experience it accordingly.[6] But using

---

6   Immanuel Kant, *Prolegomena* [1873], ed. G. Zöller and P. Lucas (Oxford: Oxford University Press, 2004), Part II; cf. Adrian Moore, *The Evolution of Metaphysics* (Cambridge: Cambridge University Press, 2012), p. 120.

this kind of lens analogy for a religious worldview would imply that we necessarily *have* to view or interpret the world in a certain way, the way suggested by a religious perspective. Yet it is obvious that this is not so. Many people start off with a religious outlook, perhaps inherited from parents and teachers, and then come to discard it (just as, conversely, there are cases of agnostics or atheists who change from a neutral or anti-religious to a religious worldview). So there is nothing necessary or unavoidable about interpreting or experiencing the world in a religious way.

We therefore need a better model for what a religious world picture is like, a model that presents it not as a pair of spectacles that cannot be taken off, nor on the other hand as an object or item in the gallery that is simply there in front of us to be scrutinized and evaluated. We need to find room for the idea that a religious worldview can be adopted or rejected, but we also need to do justice to the thought that such adoption or rejection is not a 'flat' process of detached inspection and assessment, but something more dynamic, something that engages us at a deeper level of involvement.

2. The double helix

To make progress here, I suggest we return to the idea of a 'transformative vision', which was broached towards the end of Chapter 1. We there saw Seamus Heaney's idea of poetry as offering a *transformative vision of reality*, one that is 'more than just a printout of the given circumstances of its time and place', but which somehow 'outstrips' the observed conditions.[7] What is evidently true of poetry – that it can bring about a 'transformative vision of reality' – may also in a certain sense be true of religion. Comparing religion with poetry may at first seem dubious, since

---

[7] See above, ch. 1, section 4.

the poet is a creative artist, whereas religion is generally taken to be concerned with a true account of reality, not with an imaginative creation. But the sharp contrast presupposed in this kind of objection is mistaken, since the poetical imagination is not just a 'fictive' faculty, but can be a powerful vehicle for conveying vivid and illuminating truths about the world. In other words, it can bring into focus genuine features of reality that were occluded in the more pedestrian and down-to-earth ways of looking at things. And once that is accepted, we may be a little closer to seeing how a religious outlook may involve a similarly 'transformative' vision of the world, one that discloses for the first time genuine features of reality, casting light on what was previously hidden.

But the process of coming to accept such a vision of reality is not only transformative in the sense of changing what is seen, or disclosing what was not seen before. It is also transformative in the sense that it changes the *experiencing subject*, altering the way in which she is able to see things. In other words, the transformation involved when a religious worldview is adopted is a *dual transformation*: not only does a whole new reality come into view, not only is the world, as it were, transfigured, but the subject who experiences that world is also made new. One might say, following the famous image of William Blake, that the 'doors of perception' are cleansed.[8] And this is not just an epistemic change, a change in our ability to discern or know certain things, but it is also a *moral* change, a change in the character and dispositions of the perceiver – indeed, the two types of change are inextricably linked.

It follows that such a process, unlike the more routine types of belief formation discussed in the previous section, is a highly dynamic one. Unlike the involuntary mechanisms that automatically generate my belief that there is a table in front of

---

[8] William Blake, *The Marriage of Heaven and Hell* [1790].

me when I open my eyes, or the 'flat' process of deciding what to believe, when I dispassionately evaluate the evidence and come to a conclusion, I am instead caught up in an upward *double spiral of change*, or an interacting double helix, if you will. The world starts to look different, and simultaneously my character, as I confront the world, starts to undergo a radical shift.

Now it might seem that this leads to a vicious circle, or, to put it another way, that I could never gain any entry point into the upward spiral in the first place. If I have to undergo interior change in order to accept a certain worldview, or in order to begin to discern something of what it discloses, how will such necessary interior change be possible at an earlier stage, before the transformed vision or the world has already begun to work on me? Perhaps I already have to be a certain kind of person in order for the vision to be available, or in order for such a vision to take a grip on my imagination; while, conversely, if I am not such a person, then the vision could never take hold of me in the first place. If this is right, it begins to look as if the world is going to be divided into two groups of people: those whose lives are imbued and informed with a certain picture of reality, or who are perhaps, in Wittgenstein's phrase, 'held captive' by it, and those who are outside the charmed circle, and have no way of breaking into it.

On this kind of account of the difference between believers and non-believers, there is nothing much that either group can do to change. To put the matter in the way some theologians have understood it, there will be the 'saved', already predisposed and predestined to believe and accept the true worldview, and the 'damned', whose 'hearts are hardened' and who could never come to believe.[9] How then can anyone break into the 'upward spiral' of belief? The answer given by those who take a strict 'predestinarian' line is that no one can, unless already divinely

---

[9] Cf. John Calvin, *Institutes* [*Christianae religionis institutio*, 1536].

Is it that we choose to be "saved" not that we are chosen?

so predisposed. On this view, salvation cannot be earned, and religious belief cannot be attained by any voluntary process of evaluating the evidence or scrutinizing the facts – or indeed any other human voluntary activity – but can only come as a free, unmerited gift, by divine grace.

Sad

Questions about predestination and the operation of grace have generated fierce and complicated theological debates over the centuries. For present purposes, however, we can pursue our reflections on the psychology of belief formation without being drawn into such theological niceties. The metaphor of the 'upward spiral' or 'double helix', introduced a moment ago, suggests that the adoption of a belief system or a worldview is not a matter of simply coming up against a religious belief system and then straightforwardly assenting to it or rejecting it. Rather, it may involve successive stages of transformation, both in the subject and in the way the relevant picture of reality takes shape.

To make this clearer, let us go back to the 'picture gallery' metaphor we were using earlier, but this time consider not one of the paintings hung on the wall, but a prism, fashioned of stained glass and suspended from a cord high up in the middle of the room. Many visitors ignore it or give it a wide berth, hurrying past to inspect the individual paintings. But others, without perhaps quite knowing why, linger and find themselves moving near it or standing under it. Once the resistance to moving in that direction has been set aside, the room begins, from this position, to look different. Patterns of light and colour in the air and on the walls become visible and begin to glow and shine, in turn bringing about changes in the attitude of the subject. The subject ceases to be a detached spectator, bent on inspecting and assessing the various objects in the gallery, and starts to be *moved*: responsive feelings of delight and awe begin to surface. There has, in short, been a distinctive change from an *epistemology of detachment* to an *epistemology of receptivity and involvement*. From the new vantage point, all manner of objects in the room are illuminated by the prism, bringing into focus complex new relationships, which begin to form a wondrous pattern. The meaning of the whole exhibition, before occluded, now comes vividly into view.

Without labouring the simile, which like all similes cannot be pushed too far, it may at least indicate a possible way out of the impasse described earlier – the problem of there being no way to break into the 'upward spiral' of belief. What begins as a mere minimal willingness to pause and look around becomes, as the transformations take effect, an attentive looking, and then a delighted looking; at each stage, richer dimensions of reality come into focus. As we progress up the spiral of committed attention, we ourselves undergo interior change, and this leads to changes in perception, awareness of new relationships, which in their turn generate further transformations, both in the reality that is presented to me, and in how I perceive its meaning.

But it is important to note that such a process cannot take place on a purely psychological and cognitive level. For a religious worldview is not simply a way of perceiving the world – it is a creed that demands certain active responses from me, in my behaviour and my way of living. So the spiral of belief – acquiescence, change, further perception, further change – needs at every stage to be continuously reinforced and cemented through appropriate changes in my *actions* and habits of life. To this crucial practical dimension involved in the adoption of a religious worldview we will now turn.

3. The dimension of praxis

To explore how 'praxis', the adoption of certain regular habits and modes of behaviour, is intimately involved in the adoption of a certain world picture, it may be helpful in the first instance to look at the reverse process – the case where a vision disintegrates and is lost. We have spoken of an 'upward spiral' as certain beliefs and perceptions take hold, but human life is such that in addition to an uplifting ascent, there can also be a debilitating decent as a vision fades. An example of the latter (though not one that makes any explicit reference to a religious context) can be found in Mark Twain's description of a decisive shift in his view of the Mississippi River:

> A broad expanse of the river was turned to blood; in the middle distance the red hue brightened into gold ... where the ruddy flush was faintest, was a smooth spot that was covered with graceful circles and radiating lines, ever so delicately traced; the shore on our left was densely wooded, and ... and high above the forest wall a clean-stemmed dead tree waved a single leafy bough that glowed like a flame in the unobstructed splendor that was flowing from the sun ... But a day came when I began to cease from noting the glories and the charms which the moon and the sun and the twilight wrought upon the river's face ... All the value any feature of it had for me now was the amount of usefulness it could furnish toward compassing the safe piloting of a steamboat.[10]

The narrator's enraptured vision of the delicate beauty of the flowing water and the sunlit woods that surround it seems at first so vivid and powerful that nothing could disrupt it. But as he is progressively worn down by the demanding daily chores of navigation, these wondrous aspects of the river simply cease to become salient. 'The glory and the freshness of a dream' (to borrow the language of William Wordsworth in a similar context)

---

[10] Mark Twain, *Life on the Mississippi* [1883].

finally 'dies away and fades into the light of common day'.[11] The reality has not changed, nor have the narrator's perceptual faculties been disabled; the difference has come about through action – as a result of the daily and weekly routines that are now part of his life, and which have subtly but inexorably reconfigured his orientation towards the world.

There are many lessons here. We sometimes like to think of ourselves in the position of wholly autonomous and detached evaluators, scrutinizing various pictures of the world and deciding which of them merits our assent. But the reality is that we are, from our conception onwards, biologically embodied creatures, not only subject to all the physical processes which that implies, but also, as we grow and learn, shaped and formed by what we and others do – by the patterns of behaviour into which we are inducted by the demands of upbringing, and later of education and employment. We human beings are 'always already' (to use an irritating but apt Heideggerian phrase) located in an embodied world of context and action.

It follows from this that our entire inquiry about 'how to believe' – about the ways of forming a belief system or a view of the world – needs to be understood as involving intrinsic reference to action as well as cognition: *it is an inquiry about practice as much as about theory*. To the ancient puzzle known as Zeno's paradox – how can Achilles ever overtake the tortoise? (since by the time he has covered half the gap between them the tortoise will have moved a little beyond its original position, and so on *ad infinitum*) – a time-honoured answer is *solvitur ambulando* ('it is solved by walking').[12] Do the experiment, run the race, and it's

---

[11] William Wordsworth, 'Ode: Intimations of Immortality from Recollections of Early Childhood' [composed 1804, first published 1807, full title added 1815].

[12] Compare Robert MacSwain, *Solved By Sacrifice: Austin Farrer, Fideism, and the Evidence of Faith* (Leuven: Peeters, 2013), p. 227.

glaringly obvious that Achilles can in a few strides swiftly walk past the tortoise and win the race. The analogous thought in the religious case might be somewhat as follows. Deciding on whether to accept a theistic worldview cannot be a purely intellectual decision made at a safe distance from the context of life and action. So instead of agonizing about how you could break into the 'upward spiral' of belief unless you are already predisposed to accept certain aspects of the relevant belief system, why not 'run the experiment' and start imitating the actions and practices of the believer, and see if that makes any difference.

The basic idea here was suggested many centuries ago by Blaise Pascal, who remarked that those who wanted to 'cure themselves of unbelief' should follow the practice of believers who were themselves originally in the same position: 'they are cured of the malady for which you seek a cure; so follow them and begin as they did – *by acting as if they believed*, by taking holy water, having masses said, and so on. In the natural course of events this in itself will make you believe, this will train you.'[13] Like his near-contemporary Descartes, Pascal was impressed by successful ways in which animal conduct can be modified by suitable training, and saw no reason why human beings should not, in this respect at least, be subject to similar techniques. This may seem a bit too much like brainwashing for comfort, but it is possible to interpret the Pascalian suggestion in a more sympathetic way, somewhat along the following lines.

A certain British monarch is reported to have written to his wife that he didn't love her when they were betrothed, but that he had grown to love her after many years of marriage. The bald statement may not seem the most tactful of compliments, but it has a certain integrity, and when arranged marriages were common

---

[13] Pascal, *Pensées* [*c*.1660], ed. L. Lafuma (Paris: Seuil, 1962), no. 418. Trans. in J. Cottingham (ed.), *Western Philosophy* (Oxford: Blackwell, 1996), Part V, section 6.

in royal circles, and indeed in many cultures in the world, such experiences may have been quite commonplace. They may outrage today's sentimental Hollywood-driven ideas of 'love at first sight', but may well be closer to the reality of many human relationships. For the truth is that one cannot *immediately* love someone, except in the 'infatuation' sense of being strongly attracted to him or her; genuine love implies *knowledge*, and knowledge of a person is something that necessarily grows over time. The importance of praxis, or behaviour, in this kind of context now emerges as crucial. A person's moral and emotional qualities, the qualities that have to be understood and appreciated for genuine love to take root, cannot be scrutinized at a distance as if they were an exhibit in a show – or if anyone did try to assess them in this way, it would be the shortest way of freezing or paralysing their expression. On the contrary, they have to be allowed to emerge spontaneously, in a climate of receptivity and slow nurturing. So daily actions of consideration and gentleness will be vital catalysts, allowing the possibility of a climate developing in which affection can flourish, and ripen into full love.

What holds good for the kind of awareness required for authentic love to take root may well also be true for the sensitivity required for an authentic religious outlook to take root. Certain repeated and even habitual patterns of action may be the best way of fostering the kind of focused receptivity which leads to new perceptions. And these new perceptions may in turn prompt further action, which, as it becomes absorbed in to a repeated pattern of behaviour, in turn opens the door to deeper perception. We are back with the 'upward spiral' of belief, but fortified and energized by action.

To take a concrete case, drawn from a Christian context, we may imagine the example of a doubtful or tentative believer, who may go to Church out of a mixture of feelings, but with only a faint commitment. The process of regularly hearing the gospel, and being confronted with its demands, may not produce an instant 'conversion', but, partly at a subconscious level, certain changes may occur, and slowly begin to make themselves felt. Some of these may be moral changes – for example, there may be a vague but increasing feeling of discomfort when not giving to charity, or when being less than fully honest in one's business dealings. Bringing one's conduct into line with these feelings may initially be difficult, but as it is tried, further changes will occur, and each successful occurrence of aligning one's behaviour with the moral demands now increasingly making themselves felt will further reinforce the sense that one's life is taking a new direction. This in turn will make one more susceptible to the insights that seem to provide further support for the initially tentative belief, transforming it into something that slowly moves towards the centre of one's outlook. And the consolidating of the belief gives further impetus to the process of moral and psychological change that is now under way. If all goes well, the trajectory of one's life starts increasingly to move in an upward spiral, which takes one to new insights, new moral sensibilities and a new cementing of religious belief.

None of this can be understood as a static process, or a process of merely habitual routine. If spiritual praxis degenerates into mere routine, it loses its efficacy as a catalyst for change, as the French philosopher Henri Bergson observed:

> Our inner experience shows us in habit an activity which has passed, by imperceptible degrees, from consciousness to unconsciousness and from will to automatism … Habit thus gives us a living demonstration of this truth, that mechanism is not sufficient to itself: it is, so to speak, only the fossilised residue of a spiritual activity.[14]

---

[14] Henri Bergson, *The Creative Mind* [*La Pensée et le mouvant*, 1933], trans. Mabelle L. Andison (New York: The Wisdom Library, 1946), pp. 231–2, quoted in Clare Carlisle, *On Habit* (London: Routledge, 2014).

In periods (such as much of the nineteenth and early twentieth century in England) where regular attendance at religious services was compulsory in schools and colleges, and virtually enforced by the pressures of social conformity in many ordinary communities, repeated action could lead to just the kind of 'fossilization' described by Bergson, or worse, to something analogous to the kind of downward spiral of fading perceptual vividness described by Mark Twain in the Mississippi passage. But in the right kind of praxis, where the relevant actions are performed *mindfully*, the meaning of what is enacted comes vividly alive, opening up enriched perceptions of the reality that is being confronted. In short, the vision 'takes hold' and is incorporated into someone's life as a fundamental structure that conditions how that life is interpreted and lived.

A finely nuanced description of how this kind of process can operate is provided by Clare Carlisle, taking the example of the Eucharist and its role in Christian praxis and belief:

Taking communion involves a posture of receptivity: the recipient holds out her hands to accept what the priest offers her, bowing her head in thanks, and consumes the sacrament. This posture embodies the theological idea that 'her' virtue, while genuinely hers, has its source in God. When the ritual is repeated regularly, it serves as a reminder that helps to maintain, in the lives of believers, the connection between freedom and dependence that is so central to Christian doctrine. More generally, the sacrament of the Eucharist is for Christians the ultimate expression of receptivity to God, the highest good. But it is a gesture of resistance as well as receptivity. It enacts a turning-away from more worldly or aesthetic activities: a lazy Sunday morning, the weekend papers, a game of tennis, for example. More inwardly, too, the whole process of taking communion – including the prayers that precede and follow it – involves a certain dynamic of receptivity and resistance. Since the practice will be most meaningful when it is enacted attentively, not mechanically, participants should resist the pull of distracting thoughts and try to remain present to the experience of the sacrament. This particular dynamic of receptivity and resistance combines openness and discipline: a simple openness to whatever benefits the practice may bring, and a disciplined effort to be attentive.[15]

Nothing could make it clearer that praxis, in the form of patterns of regular behaviour and action, is not a mere contingent *accompaniment* to the adoption of a worldview, nor even (as in Pascal) a useful *means* of facilitating acceptance of such a view; rather it is part and parcel of what it is to have such a worldview. It is, as it were, the very *enactment* of such an outlook in the life of the believer, something that can no more be separated from it than can the repeated patterns of action – the smiles and embraces and focused attention towards the beloved – be separated from a loving relationship. They are not accompaniments or facilitators of love, but its very embodiment.

What applies to the praxis of the ordinary believer holds good in an even more pervasive way in the praxis of those who have taken the vows of a religious order, where the disciplines of liturgy structure almost every waking hour, and are taken up into weekly and monthly and yearly routines of worship, as described in the following reflections by a Benedictine monk and theologian:

Liturgical activity transforms cosmic, historical and biological rhythms into salvation history: the night becomes a time of waiting for the Lord; the rising of the sun the

---

[15] Carlisle, *On Habit*, p. 132.

ti ... ccession of daily hours
a ... em; the end of the day a
c ... an act of abandonment in
(... onk constantly remembers
... our of himself, but that he is
... e he does not exist as a 'self'
but as a ...

The very routines of everyday life such as waking and sleeping are here transformed or 'sacramentalized' by the liturgical structures that punctuate each day. Such totality of commitment is clearly not for everyone; but it can still be argued that all religious believers – certainly in the three great Abrahamic traditions, Judaism, Christianity and Islam – are implicitly or explicitly committed to the idea of the 'sacramentality of everyday life'. The central idea here is that the religious outlook is by no means simply a matter of intellectual assent, nor even of moral orientation, but is something that is to be enacted and embodied in an intimate intermingling of belief and praxis that is in principle capable of infusing the entire tenor of a lived human life.

4. Vision and enactment

What has just been said about the 'practical dimension' involved in possessing a certain religious worldview should be a useful corrective to the tendency, particular among academics and intellectuals, to see questions about religious belief as primarily 'debating matters', topics for detached discussion. We find the various views 'interesting', and we want to dissect them and argue about them. It's not that such theological–philosophical debating is necessarily suspect – indeed, even the most committed believer

---

[16] Luigi Gioia, 'Ascetical Practices for a Secular Age', typescript, p. 3.

should be willing to admit that to take delight in using the intellect is perfectly natural and commendable – but it *can* be an evasion. As long as I remain at a safe distance, at the level of scrutinizing and evaluating the arguments and evidence, as long as I treat it as 'spectator evidence' (in the telling phrase of Paul Moser),[17] I may be shielding myself from the human vulnerability that could actually lead to a change of heart. This is surely the truth behind the Pascalian dictum that 'it is the heart that senses God, not reason'.[18]

An analogy some readers may find helpful here is that of the intellectual who has encountered certain problems in life and finds him or herself in the position of undergoing a course of psychotherapy. Professional therapists often report that intellectuals and academics are the most difficult people to treat. They will often appear on the surface to be very co-operative and motivated, and will ply the therapist with carefully thought-out questions: 'Yes, I find this Jungian/Freudian/Kleinian approach very *interesting*, but perhaps you will be able to help me clarify a few initial questions and problems which I should like to raise ...' The questions may be perfectly genuine and important ones, but there is an underlying evasion. The patient wants to stay in charge, the autonomous, intellectually gifted interlocutor, and avoid actually getting on with the painful self-scrutiny, the taxing task of opening him or herself to the discerning gaze of the other in a way that might actually require him or her to change.

In the Christian gospels there are key episodes where Jesus is described as looking directly at someone.[19] There was clearly something about that gaze that cut through evasion. The rich young man who is reported in Mark to have come to Jesus to ask

---

[17] Paul Moser, *The Elusive God: Reorienting Religious Epistemology* (Cambridge: Cambridge University Press, 2008), p. 47.
[18] *C'est le coeur qui sent Dieu et non la raison*. Pascal, *Pensées*, no. 424.
[19] Mark 10:21; Luke 22:61; John 1:42.

about the conditions for salvation was evidently prepared to have a nice debate ('Look: I've always kept the commandments, now do I, or do I not, inherit eternal life?'). As the episode is narrated, Jesus answered his question by telling him to sell everything and give to the poor. Of course there is no limit to the ingenuity of the intellectual in finding material for further discussion, and this very gospel episode can provide yet another topic for detached debate: 'Is the lesson really that Christian virtue requires total sacrifice, or is there a sufficient degree of virtue that can be attained while retaining the responsibilities we all have to discharge in normal daily life …?' But that can be just another evasion, another opportunity for detached intellectual debate – there is the possibility for endless postponement. Yet a glance back at the text itself reveals that the episode is presented in disconcertingly direct terms, and is not primarily about 'moral theory' or 'virtue ethics' at all. In the key passage that introduces Christ's response to the questioner, we are told that 'Jesus looked at him and loved him'. The clear implication is that the loving and compassionate gaze of the Other made future evasion impossible, and so the young man 'went away sorrowful'.[20]

One moral of all this is that when we are talking about 'adopting a religious worldview' it may be a kind of fetishism to insist that this must   of assent to certain specified   nce of Jesus' divine status, or tl   Quran. For if there is one clear n   hamic faiths, it is that the religiou   doxastic one (that is to say, not a   ), but always involves seeing the   to *change*. To accept the terms o   hat one is required to alter one's l   of confrontation with uncompromising standards that we did not create.

[20] Mark 10:21.

This brings out a crucial feature of what we have been calling a 'religious worldview'. We have spoken of a certain 'outlook' or 'vision of reality', but the kind of vision implied by theistic religion is not simply a descriptive account of how things are. It is in part a 'normative' vision, to use a prevalent term in contemporary philosophy – it carries with it the idea of an authoritative requirement or set of requirements. The religious vision characteristically implies the idea of a 'moral gap', as the theologian John Hare has called it, a gap between how we are and how we ought to be.[21] The vision is of a reality that is not yet fully accomplished, but against which we measure our own accomplishments and find them wanting. This latter idea is one that has a strong intuitive appeal for anyone who believes in objective moral standards, whether or not they subscribe to a theistic outlook. Thus the American moral philosopher Russ Shafer-Landau writes, 'We humans have created for ourselves a number of different sets of conventional moral standards, but these are never the final word in the moral arena. The flaws and attractions of any conventional morality are rightly measured against a moral system that human beings did not create.'[22] That seems right; but the very fact that reality is such as to impose systematic requirements on us in this way – the very fact that it confronts us with standards against which our own conventions and behaviour have to be measured – all this seems strikingly consistent with a theistic vision of the cosmos.[23]

[21] John Hare, *The Moral Gap: Kantian Ethics, Human Limits and God's Assistance* (Oxford: Clarendon, 1996).

[22] Russ Shafer-Landau, 'Ethics as Philosophy: A Defense of Ethical Non-Naturalism', in *Metaethics After Moore*, ed. Mark Timmons and Terry Horgan (Oxford: Oxford University Press, 2006), p. 22.

[23] See J. Cottingham, 'Intuition and Genealogy', in S. G. Chappell (ed.), *Intuition, Theory, and Anti-theory in Ethics* (Oxford: Oxford University Press, 2015), ch. 1, pp. 9–23.

For the religious believer, at all events, the picture will be of an enduring and eternal moral reality that requires us to change. This is not a kind of abstract requirement, but is seen by the theist in uncompromisingly direct and personal terms: each of us has to be prepared to hold our lives up to the scrutiny of a God of unsurpassable goodness and justice. And even to think about this is to see at once that we cannot withstand that gaze: 'no man can see God and live', as the Hebrew Bible puts it.[24] The specifically Christian take on this is of course that we need a Saviour, an advocate – not simply a Law, or a Holy Book, but a person who shares our human weakness, yet who is an image or icon (in St Paul's phrase) of the invisible God.[25]

But once again, this can remain a mere theoretical set of claims, unless it is supported by praxis and enactment. In the Catholic Mass, when the priest looks the communicant straight in the eye, and says, holding up the Host, 'The Body of Christ', each recipient takes the Host in total awareness of his or her weakness and failure, but in solidarity with all those fellow communicants lining up to receive the sacrament, learned or ignorant, theologically erudite and those with the haziest of beliefs if any, who, in the same direst need, acknowledge their vulnerability and dare to accept the gift that is offered. It is in this sense, for the Christian believer, that Christ is the vehicle of salvation. At the intersection of heaven and earth, symbolized by the vertical and the horizontal limbs of the Cross, we have finally stopped disputing and debating, and begun to turn in faith and hope towards the possibility of redemption.

These are very specifically Christian images, and their very specificity may seem objectionable to some critics, but exploring Christian modes of praxis need not imply any dismissal of other ways of coming to terms with the human condition and with our

---

[24] Exodus 33:20.
[25] Colossians 1:15.

need for our lives to be re-aligned towards the good. We shall return to problems of specificity in the next chapter, but for the present the argument is simply about ways of coming to adopt a religious outlook, and the need for such adoption to be realized not just in theoretical assent, but in enactment and praxis. And once this step in the argument is accepted, we are inevitably drawn to the concrete and the specific, for *there cannot be action without specificity*.

Our embodied needs as human beings are relevant here. We looked a moment ago at how, in a Benedictine community, the time-honoured patterns of prayer and worship that structure the life of a believer are woven into the rhythms of the day; we find a similar structure in the Islamic call to *salat*, the obligatory prayers performed five times a day, before sunrise, at midday, late afternoon, after sunset, and between sunset and midnight. The rhythms of day and night, or work and rest, of rising and retiring, are thus woven into the practice of worship, so that it becomes more than a theoretical set of beliefs, and is incorporated into a pattern of living. And in a similar way, the rhythms of the year, the darkness and silence of winter and the bursting out of new life in spring, are interwoven into Christian praxis, so that the message of salvation is enacted in the rituals of Christmas and Easter. An ancient ritual, still observed in some Christian communities, marks the end of the long winter and the hope of new life by the lighting of a brazier outside the Church at the vigil Mass on the eve of Easter Sunday. In the silence and the cold of night the people gather, and the light is kindled that will be used to light the Pascal candle. As the flicker of light enters the darkened Church, the cantor intones '*Lumen Christi*', 'the Light of Christ', and the response rings out '*Deo Gratias*', 'Thanks be to God!'

Such enactments are more than the sum of their parts. Their faithful performance does not in itself make true the belief system that its adherents subscribe to, but it conveys the meaning of that belief system more directly and vividly than any abstract theorizing could do. Yet the praxis has to be authentic, capable of being enacted in a dignified, sincere and mindful way. We may see how easily this can fade or go wrong when we look at how the poet John Betjeman talks of the rituals of Christmas:

> And is it true? and is it true?
> The most tremendous tale of all,
> Seen in a stained-glass window's hue,
> A Baby in an ox's stall?
> The Maker of the stars and sea
> Become a Child on earth for me?[26]

Something about the sentimental image, the 'stained glass' that depicts the 'Baby in an ox's stall', fails to resonate properly. And the repeated question 'And is it true?' is, in one way, exactly the wrong question to ask, or rather, the very asking of it is a sign of the loss of authenticity in the praxis. The poem later goes on to talk of 'carolling in frosty air' and 'steeple-shaking bells', the conventional paraphernalia depicted in Christmas cards, which combines with the 'stained glass window's hue' to give us a vague warm and comfortable feeling. It would be unfair to say that the poet mistakes the paraphernalia for the reality – indeed the close of the poem explicitly says that none of it can compare with the 'single truth' of the Incarnation (*if*, the poem adds, it is indeed true).[27] So it is not a question of impugning the sincerity of the poem or the poet, but rather of pointing to a certain sentimentality in the cosy vision of Christmas night that already shows it does not represent a valid structure of spirituality.

---

[26] John Betjeman, 'Christmas', in *A Few Late Chrysanthemums* (1954).

[27] 'And is it true? For if it is ... / No carolling in frosty air / Nor all the steeple shaking bells / Can with this single truth compare – That God was Man in Palestine / And lives today in Bread and Wine.'

But why say that the 'truth question' (Betjeman's 'And is it true? and is it true?') is in one way exactly the wrong question to ask? I most certainly do *not* mean that truth is irrelevant, or that aesthetically pleasing liturgical praxis can be a substitute for truth. On the contrary, liturgy and practice would be mere acting, mere flummery, if it were not grounded in a valid conception of the nature of reality and the meaning of human life. The problem with Betjeman's question is rather that it jumps in 'up front', as it were, with an implicit demand to settle the truth question 'straight off', as a precondition for proceeding further. It is like someone jumping in ten seconds after he has met the girl of his dreams and saying: 'I must know the truth: do you love me?' The only possible answer to this would be along the lines of Bertrand Russell's reported reply when Wittgenstein, as a young man, blundered into Russell's rooms, having just arrived in Cambridge, and demanded: 'Will you please tell me whether I am a complete idiot or not?' Russell quite reasonably responded: 'My dear fellow, I don't know.'[28] The question comes too early.

More generally, to answer the truth question properly, you need first to understand the *meaning* of what is being asserted. The peremptory demand for isolated verification is a hangover from the discredited philosophy of the early twentieth century known as positivism – a kind of obsession with checking each proposition against observational evidence. Yet to truthfully answer the question of whether one loves someone, for example, one must first understand the *meaning* of love – no easy task – and of course one must also first understand and know the person in question; both these requirements may take a lot of time and effort. So it is, *mutatis mutandis*, with the truth of the Incarnation, or of any other central doctrine of Christianity, or any other faith. We may

---

[28] Reported by Russell in 'My Debt to German Learning' [1955], reprinted in *The Collected Papers of Bertrand Russell*, vol. 11 (London: Routledge, 1977), p. 108.

wish things were as simple as our modern culture supposes, where social media sites encourage people to read a few words and immediately go online to post a 'Like' or 'Dislike' symbol (a crude thumbs-up or thumbs-down sign), affirming their agreement or disagreement. But if we are proposing to accept or reject the truth of doctrines such as the Incarnation, which are supposed to encapsulate profound and complex truths about salvation, human fragility and divine love, such quick decisions are simply not possible. Something of that complexity, far more probing and hesitant than the peremptory Betjeman-style demand to answer the truth question straight off, is conveyed in an anguished Christmas meditation written by Gerard Manley Hopkins nearly a century earlier:

> Moonless darkness stands between.
> Past, O Past, no more be seen!
> But the Bethl'em star may lead me
> To the sight of Him who freed me
> From the self that I have been …
> Now beginning, and alway:
> Now begin, on Christmas day.[29]

In the darkness of a wasted past, the speaker sees a glimmer of light which shows the road to be taken. And this finally brings us back full circle to our theme of the importance of praxis. The kinds of religious practice we have been discussing in this chapter are not just decorative or incidental embellishments, but have the vital function of deepening our understanding, not just on an abstract

---

[29] G. M. Hopkins, 'Moonless darkness', 25 December 1865, text slightly adapted in line with the splendid choral setting by Bob Chilcott (2003). Compare C. Phillips (ed.), *Gerard Manley Hopkins: The Major Works* (Oxford: Oxford University Press, 2002), p. 77.

intellectual level, but by infusing themselves into deeper layers of our moral and spiritual awareness, like clarifying crystals that sink slowly down into the depths of a murky sludge, purifying, refining, and letting in the light. Pushing the analogy yet further, we may think of the crystals as producing a real chemical change – the mixture is not just clarified but its molecular structure is radically transformed. Such an image hints at how religious belief may develop and grow when it is embodied and realized in a living pattern of spiritual praxis that engages and transforms us physically, psychologically and above all morally. For authentic liturgy is not a freely spinning wheel that looks pretty, but a form of practical enactment that orients us towards the moral demand referred to earlier – the demand to change. Authentic religion, in short, demands a response of us, and it provides a continuing structure of practical enactment that facilitates and sustains that response. If it fails to do this, then it is simply not a live option but has become a kind of fossilized relic – and perhaps for many of Betjeman's listeners it had already become just that, as it is for so many today.[30] But to deepen our grasp of these all-important moral and practical dimensions of religious belief, and to get a clearer idea of what it is that allows a religion to be a live option, we shall need to embark on a new phase of the argument, which will be the task of the next chapter.

---

[30] For the notion of a 'live option', see William James, *The Will to Believe* (1896).

Chapter 4

Religion as a Live Option

Es ist ein Ros entsprungen
aus einem Wurzel zart ...
Und hat ein Blümlein bracht
Mitten in kalten Winter
wohl zu der halben Nacht

[A rose tree now has blossomed
sprung from a tender root ...
Its flower opens bright
Amid the cold of Winter
In darkest depths of night.]

Traditional carol[1]

1. A secular age

The steady decline in previously established patterns of religious belief and observance in the developed Western world is a familiar fact of life. Although there have been fluctuations in the speed of the decline, and periodic remissions, if we compare our generation with our children's generation, it seems the downward trajectory has become sharply steeper in the last few

---

[1] Traditional German carol, first printed in the sixteenth century, trans. J. C.

decades. Some people, of course, welcome this as a sign that the superstitions of the past are at last being thrown off, at least in some parts of the world. Others, whose number is no means confined to those who are believers, worry that more and more now seem to be growing up with only the most perfunctory knowledge of the religious heritage that has shaped so much of Western civilization.

So why has religion, in particular Christian belief, ceased to be a live option for so many in the West today? How have we moved from a culture where rejecting belief in God was 'virtually impossible', as Charles Taylor puts it in his magisterial study *A Secular Age*, to a culture where for whole swathes of the population it is increasingly the default position?[2] As Taylor makes abundantly clear in his analysis, the probable causes are manifold and complex. But to find an entry point for the purposes of this chapter, let me single out one strand, which is highlighted in a recent study entitled *The Religion of the Future* by the Brazilian-born social and legal theorist Roberto Unger. Unger speaks of

> the difficulty that the educated classes experience in believing the narratives of Judaism [and] Christianity ... and the consequent weakening of the connection between the high and popular cultures of religion.[3]

The phrase 'difficulty in believing' doesn't quite get it right, I think: it suggests people striving to believe and not quite managing it, rather like the earnest struggles many clergymen in Victorian and Edwardian England had in dealing with the miraculous occurrences reported in the gospels, or, a bit later,

---

[2] Charles Taylor, *A Secular Age* (Cambridge, MA: Harvard University Press, 2007).

[3] Roberto Unger, *The Religion of the Future* (Cambridge, MA: Harvard University Press, 2014), p. 224.

like Mr Prendergast in Evelyn Waugh's wickedly malicious satire *Decline and Fall*:

> 'If things has gone a little differently I should be a rector with my own house and bathroom. I might even have been a rural dean, only' – and Mr Prendergast dropped his voice to a whisper – 'only I had *Doubts*.'[4]

Yet if we skip forward to the present day and think of the typical Anglican clergyman or woman in Great Britain, particularly at the upper educational end (Oxbridge chaplains and theology fellows, for example), it appears that so far from wrestling with 'Doubts', they are perfectly calm and comfortable about, for example, rejecting miracles like walking on the water, or the feeding of the five thousand, at least on anything like a literal interpretation. As for the doctrine broached in the last chapter, that of the Incarnation, it is clear that many contemporary theologians interpret the gospel accounts of the birth of Christ with some latitude, construing the story of the Virgin Birth, for example, as symbolic rather than historical, and taking the Christmas narratives in Matthew and Luke (wise men; shepherds) as purely allegorical. Even the locus itself, Bethlehem, is widely regarded as having emblematic rather than actual historical import (the consensus being that Jesus was in actual fact probably born in Nazareth).

Curiously, a *cordon sanitaire* tends to be drawn round one single miracle, the Resurrection, which is normally ringfenced from the demythologizing process. This may be for theological reasons, stemming from St Paul's insistence that without the Resurrection the whole Christian faith would be empty;[5] or more mundanely, it may be from fear of headlines like 'Shock and Horror as Vicar

---

[4] Evelyn Waugh, *Decline and Fall* [1928] (London: Penguin, 2001), Ch. IV, p. 31.

[5] 1 Corinthians 15.

Denies Resurrection!' As is well known, the unscrupulous British press is adept at spewing out synthetic outrage, a classic case being the fate of the Bishop of Durham, Dr David Jenkins, who was hounded in the 1980s for remarks that appeared to cast doubt on whether Christ physically rose from the dead.[6] Yet it may be that the press reaction reflected a general dislike of departures from traditional orthodoxy among the public, irrespective of their religious beliefs or lack thereof. Even in an increasingly secular age, many people may appear to have some residual attachment to their religious heritage; as Charles Taylor puts it, 'it's as though many people who don't want to follow want nevertheless to hear the message of Christ, want it to be proclaimed out there'.[7]

But how much adherence to the letter of the scriptural accounts does 'proclaiming the message of Christ' require? There's obviously something right about modern progressive theology: anyone but the strictest fundamentalist will find it absurd, and indeed unscholarly, to construe every statement in the Bible as an assertion of literal historical fact. Nevertheless, it turns out to be a delicate undertaking to find a halfway house between accepting the traditional narratives at face value and abandoning Christianity altogether. As Roberto Unger argues, the 'halfway house' strategy may be perilous, since once we start to expunge from the narratives any elements that are offensive to modern understanding, there is a risk that we will be left with a bland mixture of moral ideals that might just as well be expressed in the language of conventional secular humanism.[8]

---

[6] The original remark in a television programme was that the Resurrection should not be understood as a 'conjuring trick with bones'. Jenkins later explained that what he meant was that the risen Jesus did not have a 'literally physical body'. *The Independent* (London), Saturday 5 November 1994, http://www.independent. co.uk/voices/profile-the-one-true-bishop-of-durham-dr-david-jenkins-retiring-scourge-of-sacred-cows-1392030.html (accessed 22 November 2014).

[7] Taylor, *A Secular Age*, p. 727.

[8] Unger, *Religion of the Future*, pp. 224–5.

A further problem with the modernizing strategy is what Unger calls the 'gap between the high and popular cultures of religion'. The academic clergy may regard much of the gospel narrative as myth and allegory, but they are reticent about admitting this from the pulpit. So there is a kind of cognitive split that must sooner or later prove unstable. It all seems rather reminiscent of what happened to the version of utilitarian ethics purveyed by John Stuart Mill and his successors, so-called 'rule utilitarianism', which the philosopher Bernard Williams scathingly demolished by labelling it 'Government House Utilitarianism'. The idea of some of the 'rule utilitarians' seems to have been that the population at large should be taught to regard moral rules as categorically binding, while the elite secretly know they have the status of mere convenient rules of thumb, chosen because they tend in general to maximize happiness or utility. But not only does such a two-tier system of ethics do violence to our modern egalitarian ideals, but it strains integrity to instil into others the idea that moral laws like 'keep promises', or 'thou shalt not steal' are sacrosanct, when you yourself regard them as subject to consequentialist trade-offs. And so, *mutatis mutandis*, with the status of the religious narratives: there cannot be too wide a gap between the beliefs of elite theologians and those of the ordinary believer.

Yet there is obviously much more to the decline in religion than doubts about the truth of the scriptural stories. Religious allegiance is clearly about much more than assent to certain propositions based on the balance of evidence. As noted in the previous chapter, Wittgenstein spoke of how a certain picture can *hold us captive*, and this seems true *par excellence* of a religious picture of the world. But the phrase 'hold captive' has somewhat sinister overtones, and we might think instead more positively of a picture gripping our imagination, inspiring us, or exerting a powerful pull on our allegiance. This implies that it must appeal to us along a number of dimensions: in addition to not outraging our sense of what is rationally acceptable, for instance, it must also have a certain energy or power at the emotional and the imaginative levels. To go back for a moment to Charles Taylor, this may be part of the reason why he includes in *A Secular Age* extended explorations of various literary works, including the poetry of Robinson Jeffers, Thomas Hardy and Stéphane Mallarmé, among others. I interpret these discussions as not just embellishments, or as literary 'illustrations' added as an optional extra, but rather as absolutely integral to Taylor's argument as a whole, and to his philosophical defence of Christian theism.

Many analytic philosophers have signally failed to do justice to religion by treating it as an abstract set of intellectual doctrines to be dissected and evaluated in a detached and dispassionate way.[9] If we are to understand why our modern culture has rejected religion, let alone if we wish to have some prospect of salvaging it before it is irredeemably lost, we need to reconfigure our conception of religious understanding. If this could be achieved, it might turn out that the 'religion' that is being casually abandoned or furiously attacked in our contemporary culture does not in fact have much to do with authentic religious belief and practice as they have operated in the lives of very many religious adherents. Perhaps we need to take seriously the possibility that understanding the world religiously is *not* an attempt to dissect and analyse and explain it in the manner of modern science but rather a mode of engagement with, or connection with, reality as a whole. Perhaps the kind of connection that is sought cannot be achieved by the critical scrutiny of the intellect alone, but requires a process of attunement, or *Stimmung*, to use a Heideggerian term,[10] a moral and spiritual opening of the self to the presence of the divine.

---

[9] See further John Cottingham, *Philosophy of Religion: Towards a More Humane Approach* (Cambridge: Cambridge University Press, 2014). See also the Foreword to the present volume, p. x, above.

[10] See Martin Heidegger, *Being and Time* [*Sein und Zeit*, 1927], trans. J. Macquarrie and E. Robinson (New York: Harper & Row, 1962), H 137. See also George Steiner, *Heidegger*, 2nd edn (London: Fontana, 1992), p. 55.

2. The phenomenon of 'pervasiveness'

The issues just raised bear crucially on the question of what features a religious picture of the world must have in order to retain its power and energy. One such feature, as already suggested, is that it must resonate on a multiplicity of levels, including the cognitive, the emotional and the imaginative. An additional feature that seems essential is that the picture in question be what one might call *pervasive*: it must make its presence felt as a kind of background or frame of reference that conditions pretty much all our thinking in one way or another. Consider for example a famous account from the fourteenth century of how the arrival of spring in April makes people long to leave their homes and set out on various pilgrimages:

> And specially, from every shires ende
> Of Engelond, to Caunterbury they wende,
> The holy blisful martir for to seke,
> That them hath holpen, whan that they were seke.[11]

What is interesting for the present purpose about Chaucer's *Canterbury Tales* is that the author does not come across here in the Prologue or in the subsequent narratives as a particularly 'religious' writer. On the contrary, his interests, rather like those of Montaigne, writing two centuries later, are what could be described as humanistic. He is a keen observer of the foibles and oddities of his fellow men and women, and although his chosen subject is a pilgrimage to the shrine of St Thomas at Canterbury, he does not at all put a sacred or otherworldly frame around it, but, on the contrary, delights in the down-to-earth particularities of human existence and the individual human stories of those who

---

[11] Geoffrey Chaucer, *The Canterbury Tales* [c.1390; first pub. 1478], Prologue.

happen to have met up at the Tabard Inn in Southwark to set out on their journey. His focus, in short, is very much on the secular, not the sacred.

And yet, when all that is said, what we find in this extract and in many other passages in the poem are thoughts and turns of phrase that are ineradicably dyed with the colouring of a religious outlook. No writer today, even if they were a theologian or religious thinker, let alone if they were a kind of Chaucerian social chronicler, could possibly come up with a description like 'the holy blissful martyr' – a phrase that presupposes and accepts, almost immediately and without any self-conscious reflection, a whole web of religious, in this case Christian and Catholic, belief and tradition, including the sanctity of martyrdom and the 'blissful' reward that is merited by such witnesses to the faith.

I think that we can still feel the power of such a framework, even though there are certain parts of the poem that may raise eyebrows in the modern scientific age. If one looks at the line 'That them hath holpen whan that they were seke' [who helped them when they were sick], the idea that by visiting a saint's relics we can enlist their help in curing an illness is something most people now would probably find very hard to accept. Although our modern secular culture allows room for a certain amount of 'faith healing', this tends to be understood as a matter of autosuggestion or the placebo effect; for most people, their first port of call if they are sick is the doctor, not the shrine. But those who glibly infer that prayer is valueless, or that modern science has wholly replaced religion, fail to grasp what authentic religion is about. To suppose that belief in God is a kind of magical shortcut that will get you special benefits is not authentic religion at all, but superstition, or what Mark Johnston has aptly called 'spiritual materialism' – encapsulated by the grotesque experiments recently conducted in North America to check whether hospital patients got better quicker if unbeknownst to them strangers were praying for them.[12] This is not at all to disparage the practice of prayer; it is simply to point out that authentic prayer in the Christian tradition (as seen from Christ's formulation, 'thy will be done') is about orienting oneself towards the good, not about an individual securing personal advantage or successful outcomes that God denies to others who fail to supplicate for his assistance.

Another example of the 'pervasiveness' of the religious outlook in medieval England can be found in the following fifteenth-century version of a traditional Christmas carol (whose origins may go back a good deal earlier):

> Welcome be thou, heaven-king,
> Welcome born in one morning,
> Welcome for whom we shall sing,
> Welcome Yule!
>
> Welcome be ye, Stephen and John,
> Welcome Innocents every one,
> Welcome Thomas Martyr one,
> Welcome Yule!
>
> Welcome be ye, good New Year,
> Welcome Twelfth Day, both in fere,
> Welcome saints both lef and dear,
> Welcome Yule!
>
> Welcome be ye Candlemas,
> Welcome be ye, Queen of Bliss,
> Welcome both to more and less,
> Welcome Yule!

---

[12] See for example, H. Benson et al., 'Study of the therapeutic effects of intercessory prayer (STEP)', *American Heart Journal* 151-4 (2006), 934–42. For 'spiritual materialism', see Mark Johnston, *Saving God* (Princeton, NJ: Princeton University Press, 2009), p. 51.

> Welcome be ye that are here,
> Welcome all and make good cheer;
> Welcome all, another year,
> Welcome Yule![13]

Again, as with the Chaucer example, the predominant tone, despite all the saints' days that are listed, is not particularly 'religious' in the sense of focusing on doctrinal or credal components. On the contrary, it is an exuberant expression of good cheer, a song of yuletide gathering and feasting, the very term 'Yule' of course going back to pagan Nordic celebrations of the Winter Solstice. The successive feast days mark the turning year, the hope of the returning sun, and, alongside the exuberance, or perhaps bound up with it, a sense of the sacred – of our human frailty in the long northern winter and the majestic and awesome cycle of the seasons on which our life depends. But just as Chaucer's motley crowd of springtime travellers are united in a journey of Christian devotion, so the customs of yuletide welcome that appear in this carol are inscribed into a Christian calendar of sacred dates which, in the medieval world, were deeply absorbed into ordinary popular consciousness.

How many would now know that the traditional feast of St Thomas, apostle and martyr, was on the shortest day, 21 December (though it has since been moved to July)?[14] And how many of those who listen to Benjamin Britten's splendid setting of this carol at

---

[13] 'in fere': in company; 'lef': loved. Anon., fifteenth century. Printed in Joshua Sylvester, *A Garland of Christmas Carols, Ancient and Modern* (London: Hotten, 1861).

[14] This is of course not the same Thomas (à Becket) who was murdered in 1170 on the orders of Henry II, and whose shrine at Canterbury was the destination of the Chaucerian pilgrims, although he was born on the feast of St Thomas the Apostle (21 December), and died on 29 December, when his own feast is celebrated; so his commemoration forms part of the cycle of Christmas celebrations referred to in the carol.

Christmas concerts[15] would be able to specify the dates of the other feast days listed, Stephen, John the Evangelist, and Holy Innocents, or know that Candlemas is the feast of the Purification of Mary on 2 February, marking her observance of the Jewish rules for cleansing the ritual impurity which lasted forty days after a birth,[16] and celebrated in Christian tradition by the feast of candles, which gives expression to the steadily lengthening days after the solstice, and of course the *lumen Christi*, the growing light of the young Christ child, whose presentation in the Temple is simultaneously celebrated on this day? (The fact that 'Candlemas' is flagged up as an unknown word in both UK and US versions of Microsoft Word's spellchecker is a rather sobering confirmation of this fading of the Christian heritage in the contemporary Western world.)

The point of all these details is to draw attention to the fact that the age of faith was an age where religious belief and observance were woven into the everyday fabric of life. They were not, as it were, in a special compartment, having to do with a weird and questionable domain called the 'supernatural', but were beliefs and practices closely connected with the immanent, with the human and natural world. Yes, there is a powerful sense of the sacred, of the transcendent, but it is not, so to speak, an 'otherworldly' transcendence. It is a transcendence that irradiates the rhythms of human life, the darkness of winter and the returning light of spring, the human cycle of death and rebirth, and, above all, the sense of inhabiting a world where all this, despite its fearfulness, is a world to be celebrated with joy and thankfulness.

For religion to become a live option again would involve much more than intellectual argument of the kind familiar to academics (for example, the earnest and tortuous debates about whether a theistic worldview can be shown to be compatible with modern

---

[15] The setting is part of Benjamin Britten's *A Ceremony of Carols*, Op. 28 [1942].
[16] Luke 2:22–24.

physics and cosmology, or with Darwinian biology). This is not to disparage these debates, for many of the issues are important – the point is rather that a religious outlook requires not just rational respectability but practical incorporation into a way of life. And what this means is that there has to be structure, a *vehicle*, if you like, that serves as a means of expression for our sense of the sacredness of the natural and human world. This is no easy task, for a sense of the sacred, amid the pressures of ordinary life, comes to us only in occasional glimpses, in flashes of beauty in nature, in the transfiguring power of great art, or in compelling encounters with the mysterious authority of what the Danish philosopher Knud Løgstrup called the 'Ethical Demand', the demand that we often try to disregard but cannot ignore.[17]

What the structures of traditional religion do is reinforce this sense of the sacred, not, paradoxically, by trying to reduplicate it or artificially stimulate it, but rather by providing a structure of routine observance that prevents it from fading entirely into the background – from 'fading into the light of common day', as William Wordsworth put it.[18] Such liturgical structures may, to be sure, enable the individual worshipper on occasion to have overwhelming sacred or transcendent experiences, though these occasions are likely to be rare, and for many in the congregation, perhaps most, they will not be forthcoming at all. But the point of the traditional structures is not to offer the chance for a private spiritual trip, but, as it were, to 'regularize' the sense that we are at least *open* to the presence of the sacred. By patterns of ritual repetition and formalized observances, like the cycle of the saints' days

---

[17] Knud E. Løgstrup, *The Ethical Demand* [*Den Etiske Fordring*, 1956], ed. H. Fink and A. MacIntyre (Notre Dame, IL: University of Notre Dame Press, 1997). See J. Cottingham, 'Human Nature and the Transcendent'; in Constantine Sandis and M. J. Cain (eds), *Human Nature*. Royal Institute of Philosophy supplement 70 (Cambridge: Cambridge University Press, 2012), pp. 233–54.

[18] William Wordsworth, *Ode: Intimations of Immortality* [1804].

described in the yuletide carol, by the timeless repeated unfolding of the liturgical year, by the very fact that this is done in a prescribed routine, what is kept alive is precisely the background awareness that the everyday, immanent world is open to irradiation from something that can transform and transfigure it. In this way the immanent and the transcendent intersect – an intersection, as noted earlier, that is expressed in Christianity by the intersection of the vertical and horizontal lines of the Cross.[19]

The transcendence we are talking about here is very much *not* reducible to some kind of psychedelic experience that could just as easily be effected by pharmacological means, as proposed by the atheist philosopher Sam Harris, who (as we noted in Chapter 2) concedes that spiritual experiences are a valuable part of human experience, but suggests we could induce them by psychotropic drugs, thus dispensing with all the religious paraphernalia.[20] Rather, the transcendence we are reaching towards, at least as understood in the tradition of the Abrahamic faiths, inescapably involves a *moral transformation*. In a similar way, Charles Taylor speaks in *A Secular Age* of 'divine pedagogy' – the idea that 'God is slowly educating mankind, slowing turning it, transforming it from within'.[21]

It may be helpful to conclude this discussion of pervasiveness by referring to a recent experience at a conference on philosophy of religion in one of the islands of the Caribbean, where the British colonial past has left a strong legacy of Christian culture, manifest in countless ways, right down to the regional organization of the island into parishes, each one named after a saint. At the conference it was striking how many of the West Indian participants, especially the younger ones, expressed in their papers

---

[19] See above, Chapter 3, section 4.
[20] Sam Harris, *The End of Faith* (London: Simon & Schuster, 2004), ch. 7. See Chapter 2, section 2, above.
[21] Taylor, *A Secular Age*, p. 668.

an adamant rejection of Christianity, feeling it to be irredeemably contaminated by the history of European imperialism – hardly surprising given how many of those speaking were descendants of those who were forcibly shipped from Africa to endure slave labour on the sugar plantations. Christianity was for them simply not an option, and this shows that political and economic factors can be as decisive as philosophical and theological ones when it comes to the viability of a religion.

But the experience I wish to focus on concerns not this group of participants, but the liberal white academics, including myself, who had come to speak at the conference, and for whom a tour of the island was kindly organized by our hosts. We visited an Anglican church, a Methodist church, a Jewish synagogue and museum, and were not unmoved, particularly by the discrimination and persecution depicted in the Jewish museum. But as we traipsed round the various sites, becoming increasingly hot and footsore, our overall mood, which will be familiar to every Western tourist, was one where fatigue began to sap our appetite for cultural sightseeing. Yet at the end of the morning we were taken to a mosque, in a relatively poor part of the capital, where a young white-robed and bearded Imam showed us round. In sharp contrast to the standing about and desultory chatting that had gone on at the previous tour stops, we took off our shoes, entered the mosque, and listened in rapt attention and total respectful silence to his expositions of Islam.

What accounts for this hyper-deferential attitude among normally garrulous and blasé Western academics? It could have been the comparative novelty of the experience (in many parts of the world it is rare these days for infidels to be allowed inside a working mosque); or, despite the genial welcome of the Imam, it could even have been a subliminal frisson of wariness induced by the unresolved politico-religious conflicts and clashes of recent history (and as the philosopher René Girard has pointed out, violence and sacrifice have ancient human roots that are intertwined with the idea of the sacred).[22] But I think the most likely explanation is not any of this, but rather the striking sense we had that we were in the presence of a community for whom their religion was something highly precious, deeply integrated into their daily existence and sense of identity. The calls to worship, the daily and weekly prayers, the prescribed physical movements and rituals and repeated sacred phrases were, for this small minority of immigrants, not external religious extras tacked on to the rest of life, but the very cement of their lifeworld.

Such an interpretation may, of course, be mistaken – it is based on little more than a fleeting series of impressions on a brief visit – but the example may nevertheless serve to bring out what I take to be a crucial requirement for a religion to retain its status as a living force, as opposed to fading, as Christianity now appears to be doing in many parts of the West, into a declining asset. Secularism will not be reversed by abstract intellectual argument, nor, despite the value of preserving traditional forms of worship (as found in some ancient English colleges or beautiful old parish churches), will religion in the long run be able to be kept fully alive merely in a nostalgic or purely aestheticized form. In order to survive, it must retain, or regain, its role as a complete 'form of life', in Wittgenstein's sense, incorporated into modes of praxis that resonate with our deepest sense of who we are, and help shape and channel our emotions and our thoughts so as to keep us alive to the goodness and beauty of reality. It must, to borrow a phrase from Gerard Manley Hopkins, serve to 'keep men's wits warm to the things that *are*'.[23] Only by this fusion of the immanent and the transcendent can we hope to recover an authentic religious

[22] René Girard, *Violence and the Sacred* [*La Violence et le sacré*, 1972] (London: Bloomsbury, 2013).
[23] G. M. Hopkins, *To What Serves Mortal Beauty?* [1885], in C. Phillips (ed.), *Gerard Manley Hopkins: The Major Works* (Oxford: Oxford University Press, 2002), p. 167.

awareness, or, to revert one last time to Charles Taylor's analysis, only thus can we glimpse 'the point of being a human animal, and [feel] this call to transformation, starting to be educated by God'.[24]

3. Uniqueness and particularity

At this point in the argument there may be various reactions, depending on the background assumptions of the reader. Some people may resist the whole idea of trying to recover religion as a live option, and may feel that life can be satisfactorily lived entirely without the resources of religion, and without any reference to any supposed transcendent dimension.[25] But for those who feel at least some pull towards the kinds of focused spiritual activities and practices alluded to in the previous section, there may nevertheless be serious reservations about the very *specificity* or *particularity* of the options on offer. The previous paragraph referred to 'modes of praxis that resonate with our deepest sense of who we are', and spoke of focusing our emotions and thoughts so as to 'keep us alive to the goodness and beauty of reality'. This puts the matter in fairly general terms. But as soon as we begin to look at the actual institutions that claim to provide the opportunities for such practical engagement, we come up against some very specific practices and doctrines – those of Christianity, or Islam, or Judaism, or Hinduism, and so on. Is it just a matter of arbitrarily latching on to one of these? Is there not something absurd or even repugnant in the idea that out of many different and often conflicting forms of life, each conditioned by the contingencies of culture and history, one single option can really be *the* right choice, the uniquely appropriate vehicle for the authentic pursuit of great transcendent spiritual values that give value to human life?

---

[24] Taylor, *A Secular Age*, p. 668.
[25] For this position, see the discussion in Chapter 2, section 1, above.

One could, to be sure, deny that there is a unique 'right choice', and argue instead (as the British philosopher of religion John Hick notably did) that, despite their striking surface differences, all the world's main faith systems are, in different ways, approaches to the same ultimate ineffable religious reality.[26] But without going into the various philosophical and theological objections that have been raised against such a strategy, there is a psychological difficulty arising for anyone who is faced with the prospect of adopting a religious form of life from this kind of 'pluralist' perspective. The problem, in a nutshell, is one of *wholeheartedness*. For however 'universalist' and open-minded one's general outlook may be, actual religious praxis requires a specific kind of focused commitment, verbal and behavioural, doctrinal and liturgical, and such a commitment by its very nature requires entering completely into the relevant form of life, as opposed to regarding it 'from the outside', as it were, as one of many equally viable options.

That said, commitment certainly does not require intolerance, let alone hostility or aggression towards those who make different commitments. One can enter wholeheartedly into a given enterprise while at the same time respecting those who have gone a different route, and indeed there is no logical reason why that different route should be dismissed as containing no truth or value or insight whatsoever. On the contrary, if there is indeed a supreme and morally perfect creator who reaches out to humankind, then it is reasonable on certain assumptions to hope and expect that many of the resultant human responses will tend to manifest a great deal of commonality and overlap. Nevertheless, even allowing for all this, sooner or later there is the bullet that the authentic religious believer must be prepared

---

[26] John Hick, *An Interpretation of Religion: Human Responses to the Transcendent* [1989], 2nd edn (Houndmills: Palgrave, 2004).

to bite at the level of individual religious commitment. Sooner or later the believer must confront and come to terms with the idea of particularity: the idea that an eternal and transcendent source of value is supposed to have manifested itself truly and authoritatively in a very specific and particular way. And even if, in line with the general argument of this book, the primary emphasis is placed on the moral and practical (as opposed to purely doctrinal) components of religious observance, it will still have to be wholeheartedly affirmed by the committed religious practitioner that a particular form of liturgy or praxis is indeed the appropriate way, the fruitful way, the *right* way, in which to orient oneself towards that source of value.

If many people feel a strong resistance to such marked specificity, this may partly be because our prevailing conception since the Enlightenment inclines us to suppose that right understanding depends on looking in the direction of the universal and the abstract, as opposed to the concrete and the particular. Since the revolution inaugurated by Copernicus, 'Nothing Special' has in a certain way been the accepted slogan: it has become almost an entrenched dogma to insist that the cosmos has to be approached without supposing there is any special or privileged standpoint from which it is to be understood. We have learned to give up the naïve picture of the earth at the centre of things, and we now repeat the mantra that we are on a planet revolving around a very average star that is one among billions. The universe in its vastness seems *unfocused*, with no 'special points'. And so entrenched had this orthodoxy become by the mid-twentieth century that initially the very idea of the universe starting with a specific 'Big Bang' was fiercely resisted (until the evidence became too powerful to deny), because the notion of such a particular and singular origin violated the supposed 'perfect cosmological principle' – the idea of a homogenous universe with no 'special' or privileged times or places. The distinguished mathematical physicist and astronomer Fred Hoyle was among those who could not stomach the idea of such specialness and particularity – indeed, the very term 'Big Bang' was initially used by him and others as a term of disparagement. How could reality be so perversely particular in its origins?[27] Yet the orthodoxy, however entrenched, eventually had to crumble, since all the evidence increasingly pointed to the conclusion that the universe is indeed structured and formed out of a singularity. (The attempt to resist this with the idea of a 'multiverse' – an infinite plurality of supposedly 'actual' universes of which ours is but one – is arguably merely an ad hoc expedient devised simply to preserve the 'nothing special' dogma.)

Abandoning the 'nothing special' prejudice may have important implications for our view of the human race. It may allow us to take seriously the possibility that in cosmic terms we human beings, creatures with rationality and intelligence, may indeed turn out to be of extraordinary significance. Of course we are a fragile, utterly contingent species, and so far as we can see we might easily not have been here at all, had the contingencies of stellar and planetary history been different. But the universe has, nevertheless, produced us, operating in accordance with the universal laws of physics: it has, so to speak, 'zeroed in' on this particular, strange, featherless biped we call *homo sapiens* to be the bearers of that rare and precious attribute of self-conscious awareness. It is even possible – and despite energetic searches no evidence has yet appeared to the contrary – that this particular planet, the Earth, is the one unique location in the entire universe where there is life, and intelligence, and self-consciousness. In all the unimaginably vast cosmos, beings such as us, in whom the universe becomes conscious of

---

[27] The phrase 'Big Bang' appears to have been coined by Fred Hoyle in a BBC Third Programme radio broadcast of 1949. Hoyle subsequently became famous for his advocacy of the alternative, now discredited, 'Steady State' cosmology.

itself, are on any showing something remarkable, and it may even be, for all we now know, that we are unique and utterly alone.

Truly appreciating the implications of this requires us to take a step back from everything that has become orthodoxy since the Enlightenment. A picture now starts to coalesce according to which it is at least possible that reality operates not solely in terms of impersonal, universal laws, as supposed in the blank, Deistic universe of the eighteenth century, and exalted into a dogma by modern naturalism, but rather in a way that *focuses*, uniquely, individually, on particular *carriers of significance*. Just as the universe is unique, and had a unique origin in a singularity, so it is possible that life and intelligence is unique, and exists only here on Earth. If so, and it is a fearful thought, then ultimate, cosmic responsibility rests on *us*. We may resist it, but it may be an unavoidable truth that everything hinges on us, and our choices – just as, in my own individual life, on the traditional theistic picture, I have momentous, ultimate responsibility for my actions, and am finally answerable for everything I do or fail to do, whether I like it or not.

The kind of worldview we find in the theistic religions has always presupposed this focus on the particular and singular, and indeed embraced it. Thus, in the biblical narrative, a small seemingly insignificant Middle Eastern tribe becomes the special focus of divine action, and then, in the Christian story, a particular, seemingly drab and undistinguished town, Nazareth, on the remote periphery of the Roman Empire, becomes the place where the divine light appears. It outrages secular orthodoxy that anyone should suggest such singularities or particulars should have this kind of status, but, for all that, it appears, to put it no stronger, at least consistent with contemporary scientific cosmology to suppose that the universe itself is 'focused' in this way, so that reality is, so to speak, funnelled into unique channels of significance.

4. Funnels of significance

For the religious believer, the notion of reality as being structured in such a way that momentous significance resides in the particular is an idea that goes right down to the level of an individual life. This again is against the impersonalist orthodoxy that has been prevalent since the Enlightenment, for example in the utilitarian ethics of consequentialism, which has had such a strong influence on moral thinking in the last hundred years and more. The logic of consequentialism is that resources should be allocated strictly in accordance with impersonally assessed criteria, and that the right action in a given case is something to be determined impartially, by reference to how the results contribute to the general good. So in the late eighteenth century William Godwin famously argued that if one had to choose between rescuing one's mother from a burning building and rescuing someone of great worth and value to society, it would be right to rescue the latter. Why should it matter, Godwin asked, that my mother is special to me, that she is *my* mother? 'What magic is there in the pronoun "my" that should justify us in overturning the decisions of impartial truth.'[28]

But although such austere impartiality may be appropriate in certain circumstances, for example for an official in charge of distributing public funds, it can hardly be the foundation of all morality. Without the special commitments that require us to allocate very significant portions of our time and resources to those we love and care for, our lives would be immeasurably poorer – and not just because they would be psychologically less rich and satisfying, but because they would be *morally* deficient. Special concern, special affection, special commitment – these are not some unfortunate interference to the moral life; they are the

---

[28] William Godwin, *Enquiry Concerning Political Justice and its Influence on Modern Morals and Happiness* [1798], 3rd edn, ed. I. Kramnick (London: Penguin, 1985), p. 170.

very lifeblood of morality. They are the me___ ___hereby each of us, as a child, was _____ ___r it is a cliché, but a true one, that _____ ___ value oneself. By being loved, we _____ ___ love we develop the sensibilities _____ ___ us to empathize with others and ___

Getting the b_____ _____ ___en love of self, love of those clos____ _____ ___r world – is of course a complex _____ _____wers.[29] But the key point for the _____ _____nt is that our flourishing as hum_____ ___ ___ inextricably bound up with the intimate sense of specialness that sustains our own individual self-awareness, and which links us to our loved ones. Without it, we are not truly human, but mere ants in some communal utility hive.

The ethics of Christianity throw an important light on these questions. Much Christian teaching is of course concerned with widening the scope of our concern for others, and reaching out to anyone we encounter who is in need, as in the famous parable of the Good Samaritan, found in Luke's Gospel. But it is important that the story, as told in Luke, is produced by Christ as a response to the question 'Who is my neighbour?',[30] in other words, as a way of explicating the ancient and fundamental command 'love your neighbour as yourself'.[31] And as many have pointed out, this command makes no sense unless it is morally legitimate to love oneself. Once again, our very identity as moral beings depends on each individual agent being a special locus of concern and

---

[29] See further B. Feltham and J. Cottingham (eds), *Partiality and Impartiality: Morality, Special Relationships, and the Wider World* (Oxford: Oxford University Press, 2010).

[30] Luke 10:29.

[31] Christ here endorses the fundamental teaching found in Leviticus 19:18. See also Mark 12:31; Matthew 22:39.

significance, and it is only those who are securely nurtured in such self-concern who are morally equipped to love and care for others.

In an extraordinary poem by Rainer Maria Rilke, the speaker addresses God and demands how he will cope when he (the speaker) dies:

Was wirst du tun, Gott, wenn ich sterbe?
Ich bin dein Krug (wenn ich zerscherbe?)
Ich bin dein Trank (wenn ich verderbe?)
Bin dein Gewand und dein Gewerbe
mit mir verlierst du deinen Sinn.

Nach mir hast du kein Haus, darin
dich Worte, nah und warm, begrüßen.
Es fällt von deinen müden Füssen
die Samtsandale, die ich bin.

[What will you do God, when I'm done?
I am your vessel – when I'm gone?
I am your drink – when I am none?
I am the cloth you worked upon;
Me flown, your meaning all will flee.

When I am dead, no house for thee,
No loving welcome words to greet;
Nor more to soothe your tired feet
The soft warm slipper that is me.][32]

---

[32] Rainer Maria Rilke, 'Was wirst du Tun, Gott, wenn ich sterbe', from *Das Stunden-Buch* ('The Book of Hours') [1903], I, 36, first two verses. My translation departs from literal exactness in a few places but aims at reflecting the tightly structured metrical and rhyme scheme of the original.

At one level, this address to God seems oddly intimate and self-focused; yet it captures at another level that sense each individual has of the utter preciousness and uniqueness of the self – the sense in which the self is, for this transient and frail consciousness that is mine, the centre about which the rest of the universe turns. When I am gone, says the speaker, even God will be bereft and bereaved. And part of the greatness of the poem lies in the fact that this sense of specialness is somehow mysteriously justified. Each centre of consciousness has momentous value: to God, as the gospel saying puts it, even the hairs of your head are numbered.[33] So what is superficially the absurdly arrogant idea that God will be at a loss, just because this one human being among millions is no more, actually reflects a deep moral truth that the Judaeo-Christian worldview proclaims about the infinite value of the individual. That truth is conveyed theologically in the conception of God as (in the words of one commentator on Rilke's poem) 'searching for partnership and love among his own Creation'.[34] Rilke's own religious outlook underwent many shifts and ambiguities, but the depth of insight found in this poem could only have come from a writer whose moral sensibilities were pervasively shaped by the theistic tradition.

Yet to achieve full understanding of the issues raised in the poem, we must allow the pendulum of interpretation to swing back again. It *is*, after all, a piece of megalomania to suppose that God will be bereft at my passing. I may be a unique individual, but it is surely the beginning of moral wisdom to learn that each of us is but one among many, and that when one dies, *nothing much will change*. An analogous sense that one has no right to special treatment is conveyed in practical enactment, in the central Catholic liturgy of the Mass: each participant is but one among many, all in need

---

[33] Luke 12:7; Matthew 10:30.
[34] Stanley Burnshaw, *The Poem Itself* (Harmondsworth: Penguin, 1960), p. 143.

of grace, as each joins the long line of those approaching the altar to receive communion. And something similar is expressed in the *Confiteor*, the general confession that starts every Mass, where each penitent joins in the communal declaration, and not only acknowledges his sin to God – 'I confess to Almighty God ... and to all the angels and saints', but also directly addresses those around him: '... and to you, my brothers and sisters'. In a remarkable and healing way, this is an implicit rejection of specialness: there is no question of my communing with God on a self-indulgent private spiritual trip. On the contrary, it is to these fellow worshippers on either side of me, these ordinary citizens, no doubt with their down-to-earth and no-nonsense view of transgression, to whom one acknowledges that one has failed.

Participating in such an enactment requires a kind of courage – there is a requisite humility here, which can perhaps only be fully understood by someone who lays aside their 'adult' superiority and detachment, or their philosophical scruples about the coherence of the ecclesiastical doctrines involved, and actually dares to engage in the practice, acknowledging that they have no recourse but to make their plea – not into a 'caring' or specially 'sympathetic' ear, on in a privileged interview, but rubbing shoulders with the ordinary fellow worshippers around them. No one, of course, can be compelled or argued into putting themselves in such a frame of mind; the logic of the process must take over. But the obstacles to wholehearted participation in such an enactment are formidable, as may perhaps be glimpsed in an analogous case. People who have experienced the ordeal of standing trial will typically report that a major part of the ordeal is that the accused, hitherto perhaps confident of his status and security, now needs to defend himself in front of not colleagues, or family, or friends, but an anonymous jury of ordinary citizens, who do know nothing of him, who have no special sympathies for him, who are not legal or forensic experts, yet before whom his case must be tried. And as in the forensic, so in the liturgical setting, to have the courage to abandon the sense of privilege, of specialness, may be the first step along the path to moral maturity and growth. Pride is the oldest, the greatest, sin, and it is the hardest to give up.

Yet (and here the pendulum swings back once more) even when all this has been said, and even when the hard disciplines of spiritual praxis have required the abandoning of specialness, there remains something right about the perspective of Rilke's poem. For this focus of subjectivity that is *me* remains unique, and so there is located in me this momentous responsibility – to make use of this unique and precious existence that has been bestowed on me for good or ill. So I am nothing special, but also, in a crucial way, I am special. No one but me, this unique individual, has the power either to direct my life outwards in joy to the glory of God and the love of my fellow creatures, or inwards towards egoism and futility. And the implication of Rilke's verses is that God himself is searching for the fulfilment, the completion, that arises when the first of these paths is taken. So despite the existential fear of death that is clearly deeply at work in the poem (the very last line of which is 'I am afraid'), what also shines through is the sense that a life, however fragile and short, is after all redeemable if it becomes a vehicle – a 'vessel', a 'garment', a 'home' – for the sacred. So, although Rilke's own personal attitudes to religious faith were complex and shifting, it is perhaps not too fanciful to suppose that if the Rilke of this poem had been interrogated about its purpose, he might have been prepared to concur with the sentiment expressed by Dylan Thomas about his own work many years later: 'These poems, with all their crudities, doubts, and confusions, are written for the love of Man and in praise of God, and I'd be a damn' fool if they weren't.'[35]

---

[35] Dylan Thomas, Note to Author's Prologue, prefaced to *Collected Poems* (London: Dent, 1952).

The image we began with in the epigraph at the beginning of this chapter depicts a solitary rose, fragile, frail and utterly unexpected, blossoming in the darkness of a winter night. In the context of the carol from which the lines are taken, the reference is of course to the Nativity – the arrival of the Christ child whose birth, since early Christian times, has been celebrated in the deep midwinter of the year. But in the light of our explorations of individual 'specialness' in this chapter, we may also see the rose as a symbol of each human life, fragile, fleeting, yet somehow of momentous significance. In theological terms, this may connect with the idea articulated by Paul when he makes the remarkable declaration that we have all become 'co-heirs' with Christ;[36] for the appearance of the divine in ordinary human form has opened the possibility that every human being, however flawed, can be caught up into a cycle of healing and redemption. So the appearance, past all probability, of the single rose blossoming in the bitter cold of winter is not just an isolated event, but somehow conveys to all of us that we are more than accidentally arising organisms thrown out at random into the darkness of a meaningless world. The divine light that 'shines in the darkness and is never quenched'[37] offers the hope that the light of each individual human life, frail, flickering and ever at risk of extinction, can yet be of infinite worth.

---

[36] Romans 8:17.
[37] John 1:5.

Chapter 5

The Disclosure of the Sacred

Draw not nigh hither: put off thy shoes
from off thy feet, for the place whereon
thou standest is holy ground.

Exodus[1]

1. Religion and art

A calm sense of the benignity of the world is captured in a painting entitled 'View of Østerbro from Dosseringen' by the nineteenth-century Danish artist Christen Købke. It depicts a weekend outing of an ordinary family as they relax on their small sailing dingy moored near Copenhagen.[2] The mood of the painting is finely evoked by Alain de Botton and John Armstrong in their study *Art as Therapy*:

> The light in the picture is tremendously meaningful, even though it is difficult to say what this meaning is. One wants to point at the picture and say 'When the light is like this, I feel like that.' Købke has created an image that is in love with nothing happening. The child hangs over the rails, the man in a top hat looks on while his friend makes some adjustment to the bottom of the furled sail. The women say

---

[1] Exodus 3:5, King James Version.
[2] Christen Købke, *View of Østerbro from Dosseringen* (1838).

something to one another. Life is going on, but there is no drama, no expectation of an outcome, no sense of getting anywhere. Rather than this being a condition of boredom or frustration, though, it feels exactly right. It is tranquil but not tired. It is immensely peaceful but not inert. In a strange way, the picture is filled with a sense of delight in existence expressed quietly.[3]

Art is clearly capable of expressing such simple delight in existence. But it seems to me that there is something more at issue here, which de Botton and Armstrong's discussion skirts around but does not quite bring out. Is what is conveyed by the painting merely a sense of calm repose, or is there (as the phrases 'tremendously meaningful' and 'exactly right' perhaps hint at) a deeper tranquillity, a sense of being at one with the rest of creation? If it is the latter, then the feeling evoked is something akin to what has been called 'ontological rootedness',[4] a conviction that we are somehow secure or 'at home' in the world.

This calls to mind Wittgenstein's feeling of 'absolute safety',[5] which he identified with the religious outlook. But it is important that such a feeling is not confused with a belief that one has some kind of privileged immunity to trouble. Even the minimally reflective religious believer is as well aware as anyone else that at any time terrible things can and do happen to us. The God of authentic religious belief is not to be identified with some cosmic micro-manager or pagan tutelary deity who magically insulates his chosen devotees from trouble. The world is a turbulent place, full of undeserved threats and arbitrary dangers, and to try to claim that

---

[3] Alain de Botton and John Armstrong, *Art as Therapy* (London: Phaidon, 2013), p. 47.

[4] Simon May, *Love: A History* (New Haven, CT: Yale University Press, 2011), p. 6.

[5] See Chapter 3, section 1.

every ghastly accident or hideous disease has a divinely planned
'meaning' (for example as a punishment for sin, or as a warning) is
a crude distortion of the religious outlook in its more reflective and
morally sensitive forms – and indeed is explicitly repudiated both
in the Hebrew Bible (in the story of Job) and in the Christian New
Testament, where Christ makes clear his distaste for attributing
physical infirmity or natural catastrophe to moral failings on the
part of the victim.[6]

The 'safety' that is at issue, then, is not like ordinary mundane
security – the basic freedom from hunger and cold and external
interference that is a precondition for our being able to carry
out our normal human activities without risk or interruption.
Mundane security is of course vitally important, and a great deal
of our energy, together with the resources of the modern state
with its elaborate infrastructure, is rightly expended on providing
it. But once it *is* provided, we only feel all the more strongly the
enduring existential insecurity that is our human lot. We yearn
for our lives to be truly meaningful; we long to feel grounded and
validated by reference to something more than our own fluctuating
propensities and preferences. As the British philosopher Simon
May has expressed it, our very flourishing as human beings is

founded upon a lifelong search for a powerful relationship to
the ground of our being, and … whether it takes a religious
or secular form, such a search is the ultimate purpose of a
well-lived life.[7]

The phrase 'whether it takes a religious or a secular form' is
significant, since it suggests that the search for fundamental

---

[6] See the discussion of the eighteen who died in the collapse of the tower of Siloam
(Luke 13:1–5), and of the man suffering blindness from birth (John 9:3).

[7] May, *Love*, p. 256.

grounding, which is obviously the mainspring of the religious impulse, can be catered for in other ways – for example by art. De Botton and Armstrong's suggestion in *Art as Therapy* is that this is not only possible but desirable: we should, as they put it, develop 'a new post-Christian canon for art'. Their idea is that we should 'rewrite the agenda for commissioning so that art can start serving our psychological needs as effectively as it [once] served those of theology'. Art, in other words, should be co-opted into the tasks previously addressed by religion, such as helping us to achieve self-knowledge, love, forgiveness, and sensitivity to the pains of others.[8]

De Botton and Armstrong go on to speak of the 'transformative and redemptive power of art' which was 'pioneered' in churches and temples. The religious project may have 'lost its allure', they say, but museums and galleries should aim to promote the underlying values in a purely secular context. So Donatello's sculpture of the Virgin and Child ought to be placed in a gallery devoted to illustrating 'tenderness'; a fifteenth-century triptych panel by Juan de Flandes depicting the risen Christ appearing to Mary should be exhibited with a caption explaining the love and grief inherent in a mother–son relationship and exhorting men to 'understand – and call – their mothers'.[9]

If we set aside the banality of this last phrase (untypical of what is elsewhere an insightful and sensitive book), the underlying idea that art can take the place of religion in the modern age is one that may appeal to many of those who have discarded their religious beliefs, or grown up in a milieu where religion was simply not a live option. But there is a serious problem in such a position. Reducing the message of great spiritual art to secular terms may risk trivializing it, or at least losing sight of the profundity and complexity of its meaning. Thus in Donatello's sculpture of Mary

---

[8]   *Art as Therapy*, pp. 78, 80.

[9]   Ibid., pp. 92, 91.

and the infant Jesus (as with many other famous depictions of this archetypal Christian subject) mere 'tenderness' does not begin to capture the many layers of meaning involved. In the sculpture, the child, with a proleptic intensity beyond its years, gazes into the mother's face and seems to attempt to comfort her, while the woman, utterly maternal and devoted in her embrace, nonetheless looks past the child with a face riven with secret awareness and grief – for has she not just been told 'your child will be the cause of the falling and rising of many, a sign to be spoken against, and a sword will pierce your very soul'.[10] The whole point about the value of religious art is that it has to be understood within an intricate web of meaning, woven out of the profoundly resonant narratives of Scripture and the centuries of meditation and reflection that followed them. To strip out all these religious elements, leaving only the residue of a moral or therapeutic 'lesson' for a presumed audience who have had no deep immersion in the relevant form of life, is to strip out most of the meaning of the works of art that we are supposed to be understanding and appreciating.

But is it not possible for the religious elements to be re-interpreted in secular terms? This seems to be the thinking behind many modern approaches to the great Christian artistic heritage of the West. Listeners to the BBC in recent years, for example, will know that any broadcast performance of a sacred masterpiece such as Bach's *Matthew Passion* will inevitably be preceded by an announcer or continuity person bustling up to the microphone to insist that 'of course, this music is not about religion but about great human emotions and values'. There appears to be an implicit assumption here that the Christian worldview is obsolete in the modern age, so that the next step is to propose a 'post-Christian' framework, where we can focus instead on the 'drama' and

---

[10] Simeon's prophecy, Luke 2:34–35. For the presentation of the infant Christ in the Temple, where this prophecy was made, see above, Chapter 4, section 2.

the 'human values'. But there is a false contrast here. The great religious narratives, such as the account in Matthew's Gospel of the arrest, trial, torture and crucifixion of Christ, are indeed about human values – what is depicted is a drama of persecution, betrayal, rejection, violence, denial, guilt, cruelty, callousness, deep suffering, patience, sacrifice, grief, exhaustion, mourning, consolation and hope. Yet what the music of Bach supremely conveys, and it is music that is inextricably bound up with the religious faith from which it sprang and which it expresses, is that this human drama has an eternal, an archetypal, significance. The words and the music plumb the depths of human pain and futility, but in doing so lift them up, in every note and cadence, to transfiguration and redemption.

So it is not a case of '*either* religious *or* human'. Rather, to see this agonizing yet wonderful story in the way that is illuminated by this masterpiece is to see the profoundly human drama as infused, from first to last, with religious significance. To be sure, those who respond to the fusion of words and music in all the complex and deeply felt ways that it demands may not necessarily wish to sign up to all the credal doctrines of Christianity; they may even explicitly declare, as many celebrated modern interpreters of such great sacred music often do if asked, that they are not themselves believers. But in responding to the drama in the way they do, with complete dedication and devotion and awe, they are implicitly showing that it is for them more than merely 'aesthetically' or 'musically' valuable, though of course it is both; they are showing that it reaches a dimension that entirely transcends the merely technically outstanding, or intellectually rewarding, or emotionally enriching. It has a deeper resonance, stemming, to be sure, from our human struggles and needs, but somehow reaching beyond them and engaging those indefinable and all-important longings that we call, for want of a better term, 'spiritual'. When such music takes possession of us, we are on that mysterious threshold that beckons us forward yet at the same time carries a warning that to cross it will be to abandon the whole reassuring world of secular certainty and human self-sufficiency: we have reached the threshold of the sacred.

2. Crossing the threshold

We are now in territory where philosophical definition is difficult, but most of us can point to moments in our lives where we have felt ourselves approaching the threshold of the sacred. Not all may accept the label 'sacred', since they may wish to distance themselves from any religious implications, but in human and experiential terms at least it seems clear that the phenomenon is widespread. For some it may happen before uplifting works of painting or sculpture, for others when they are confronted with the breathtaking beauty of a natural landscape, for others in the overwhelming emotion generated by a great work of music, where we sense 'a bottomless chasm in the scheme of things, a falling away into the transcendental, and ourselves as poised on the edge'.[11] This sense of ourselves as 'poised on the edge' (the phrase is Roger Scruton's) points us to something important about the sacred in all its manifestations. One might express this by saying that what is brought into view is not just an object with such-and-such properties, but a special kind of meaning as disclosed to the experiencing subject.

Considered as a subject of conscious experience, a human being is not reducible to the objective world of things and processes studied by science. As Martin Heidegger put it when in referring to a human being he used the term *Dasein* (literally 'being there'),[12] each of us is a unique centre of consciousness that is mysteriously

---

[11] Roger Scruton, *The Face of God* (London: Continuum, 2012), p. 160.
[12] Martin Heidegger, *Being and Time* [*Sein und Zeit*, 1927], trans. J. Macquarrie and E. Robinson (New York: Harper & Row, 1962).

'there', thrown in to the world, confronted by the mystery of existence. So there is a sense in which even our ordinary presence in the world is a source of wonder. But the dimension of the sacred involves far more than this. Much of this world that we are thrown into we have to 'deal with' in order to survive: our day-to-day needs, for food, for shelter and much else besides, require us to make use of the things we encounter in all sorts of ways. But when we approach the threshold of the sacred, these ordinary mundane needs are temporarily put aside. We no longer confront reality as tool-bearers, or biological exploiters or technological manipulators; time seems to be frozen, and we are overwhelmed with a stillness, an awe.

An encounter with the sacred calls us to suspend the instrumental attitude that treats everything as a commodity to be used. The crucial thing about a response of awe, a genuine sense of the sacred, is that there is something that seems to say 'keep off!', as in Moses' encounter with the burning bush in the Exodus story, quoted in our opening epigraph, where he is told not to approach too near. This sense of our normal busy human enterprises being somehow checked or halted seems to be something that contemporary secular reductionist accounts of the sacred have missed, or at least not fully taken on board. The 'new atheists' are keen to proclaim that they too enjoy beautiful sunsets as much as any theist, and Richard Dawkins has even declared (on what possible scientific evidence is not vouchsafed) that the precise selfsame impulses that led poets like William Blake to mysticism 'lead others of us to science'.[13] But while it is obviously true that experiences of wonder at the beauty of nature, or of great art, can come to everyone irrespective of religious allegiance or its lack, there is far more

[13] Richard Dawkins, *Unweaving the Rainbow* (London: Penguin, 1998), p. 17.

to such experiences than simply saying 'wow' when you watch the sun dipping below the horizon.

To understand the sacred properly is to understand its obverse side – the possibility of desecration – a point that has been well brought out by Roger Scruton when he observes that 'the rearranging of the world as an object of appetite obscures its meaning as a gift'.[14] Had Moses blundered in and trampled on the holy ground, he would have blinded himself to its significance, just as we do nowadays as tourists, when we elbow our way into historic churches and temples to chatter away and check out the exhibits in our guide books, or worse, do not even bother to look around, but immediately pull out our iphones so that we can upload our pictures on to a social media website. In our modern, secularized world, the eagerly sought but ultimately wearisome experience of 'sightseeing' has become a mere commodity, and in purchasing it not only do we desecrate the holy, but we desensitize ourselves.

In *Paradise Lost*, Milton plays on an ancient etymological connection between the holy and the accursed (in Latin *sacer*), when Adam calls the fruit of the forbidden tree 'sacred': *that sacred Fruit, sacred to abstinence*.[15] It was sacred precisely because it was *set apart* from the other fruits of the garden, the one they were not to touch; in failing to keep off, they made it accursed – its taste, as Milton puts it, bringing 'death into the world, and all our woe'.[16] The true sense of awe that is the basis of the religious impulse, here as elsewhere, is not (as it is sometimes mistakenly or maliciously represented as being) a superstitious servility towards an arbitrary

[14] Scruton, *The Face of God*, p. 177. For more on the notion of gift, see Chapter 2, section 4, above.

[15] John Milton, *Paradise Lost* [1667], Book IX, lines 921–5: 'Bold deed thou hast presum'd, adventrous *Eve* / And peril great provok't, who thus hath dar'd / that sacred Fruit, sacred to abstinence / Had it been onely coveting to Eye / Much more to taste it under banne to touch.'

[16] *Paradise Lost*, Book I, line 3.

and tyrannical divine command, but rather a recognition that there is a dimension of reality that demands our respect – a value that confronts us whether we like it or not, that calls us to refrain from grabbing and grasping, and which is not simply *there* for us to control and commodify.

A vivid sense of the sacred is expressed in many scriptural passages, including some that use language whose focus we would probably classify (in our somewhat impoverished modern vocabulary) as 'aesthetic' or 'moral', as in the following verses from a well-known Psalm:

> Let the heavens be glad, and let the earth rejoice: let the sea roar, and all it contains.
> Let the field exult, and all that is in it: then all the trees of the forest will sing for joy
> Before the LORD, for he comes, he comes to judge the earth: he will judge the world in righteousness, and the peoples in his faithfulness.[17]

God is here not an immaterial force that is supposed to *explain* the behaviour of the oceans and fields and the woods; rather, the vivid beauty and splendour of the natural world is that which *makes manifest* the divine. The world is understood *religiously* – not as a blank impersonal process, not as A. E. Housman's 'heartless witless nature',[18] not as a manifestation of 'blind, pitiless indifference', as Richard Dawkins characterizes it,[19] but as 'charged with the grandeur of God'. This is the vision powerfully expressed by Gerard Manley Hopkins when he speaks of all things as being 'charged with love ... charged with God, [so that] if we know how

[17] Psalms 96[95]:11–13.
[18] In 'Tell me not here, it needs not saying', *Last Poems* (1922).
[19] Richard Dawkins, *Rivers Out of Eden* (New York: Basic Books, 1995), p. 133.

to touch them [they] give off sparks and take fire, yield drops and flow, ring and tell of him'.[20]

The feebleness of modern labels like 'aesthetic' for the type of language found in the Psalm just quoted is even more apparent in an earlier Psalm, where God is described as the one who 'breaks the cedars of Lebanon and makes Lebanon skip like a calf', who 'shakes the wilderness and strips the forests bare, while all in the temple cry "Glory"'.[21] The cry of 'Glory' (in Hebrew *kavod* בָּכוּד) signifies something weighty with significance, sacred, mysterious, a manifestation of the divine, as conveyed in the description of the pillar of fire and cloud which led the Israelites out of Egypt, or the cloud atop Mount Sinai, where God's law was manifest to Moses.[22] We are not talking of 'natural beauty' in the attenuated modern sense, but of something fearful that calls forth reverence and awe, like the burning bush, flaming but never consumed, where Moses was told to keep his distance.[23] These are not 'impressive sights' of the kind familiar from television nature programmes, but events pregnant with moral significance, as is clear from the lines in the earlier Psalm quoted, where the forests 'sing for joy' not just in pantheistic exuberance, as it were, but rather because *the world is to be judged*. In psychological or phenomenological terms, what is happening here is an experience where the subject is overwhelmed by the power and beauty of nature in a way that is somehow intertwined with awareness of one's own weakness and imperfection, and a sense of confrontation with

[20] G. M. Hopkins, *Note-books and Papers*, ed. H. House (Oxford: Oxford University Press, 1937), p. 342; cited in *The Poems and Prose of Gerard Manley Hopkins*, W. H. Gardner (ed.) (Harmondsworth: Penguin, 1953), p. 231. Compare Hopkins' famous poem that begins 'The world is charged with the grandeur of God', from *Poems (1876–1889)*.

[21] Psalm 29[28]:5–9.

[22] Exodus 13:21; 16:10; 24:16.

[23] Exodus 3:5.

the inexorable demands of justice and righteousness. The 'religious understanding' involved here is, in short, the kind of awareness that enables one to see the world transfigured, so that it is irradiated with meaning and value, and the human subject, caught up in that mystery, is unmistakeably called on to be no longer a spectator, a mere 'tourist', but to *respond*, to be a morally responsive agent, part of a cosmos that is *diaphanous*, transparent to the divine.

3. The sacred secularized?

It would be inept to dismiss phenomena of this kind as mere made-up stories or fabrications – they clearly correspond to *something* within the wide and varied spectrum of human experience. But does that 'something' have to be characterized in religious terms? Some have argued that it can be accounted for as an aspect of human experience that is in principle explicable scientifically and without any reference to the divine. The atheist philosopher Sam Harris, whom we have had occasion to mention earlier,[24] has claimed that what is valuable about spiritual experience can be understood, and its value preserved, provided we are prepared to jettison the irrational accretions stemming from religious belief, particularly those of the Abrahamic faiths, where feelings of awe of the kind just discussed are bound up with superstitious and unscientific fears about a supernatural being who demands our allegiance. For, according to Harris, 'the central message of [Judaism, Christianity and Islam] is that each of us is separate from, and in relationship to, a divine authority who will punish anyone who harbors the slightest doubt about His supremacy'.[25]

---

[24] See above Chapter 2, section 2, and Chapter 4, section 3.
[25] Sam Harris, *Waking Up: A Guide to Spirituality without Religion* (London: Bantam Press, 2014), p. 21.

But does a religious approach to the sacred stem ultimately from primitive feelings of terror before a harsh and punitive God? There are several issues that need to be disentangled here. The first is the question of whether the God of the Abrahamic faiths is indeed a punitive and terrifying authority who demands allegiance. And here we must acknowledge that the evidence from Scripture is mixed: there are evidently texts that point in that direction, speaking of an apparently ruthless and implacable God,[26] while others tell a different story, as in Hosea's proclamation of a God who desires 'mercy not sacrifice' – a text invoked by Jesus of Nazareth.[27] There are, of course, fundamentalists who insist that every single word and sentence of Scripture must be taken in an uncompromisingly literal way, but most textual scholars would regard scriptural interpretation as a far more nuanced and complicated matter than that. And in any case there are many believers who are perfectly prepared to accept that humanity's religious awareness is something that develops and matures over time (just as we hope and expect our moral and scientific awareness will grow). And if the nature of God is progressively grasped and progressively revealed as humanity develops, there is something odd and disquieting about the way in which the critics of religious faith in our contemporary culture so often insist on underlining those ancient texts that appear to place religion in the worst light.

That said, it's important to be wary of the simplistic contrast, often drawn in Christian apologetic writing, between the harsh God of the 'Old Testament' and the loving 'Christian' God of the New. As much recent scholarship has shown, there are strong continuities between the teachings of Jesus of Nazareth and the Jewish moral and religious tradition from which he sprung and of which he is an inextricable part. And in any case, the idea

---

[26] See for example Joshua 9:24.
[27] Hosea 6:6; Matthew 9:13.

that the God depicted in the 'New Testament' is a God of wholly unconditional love is in fact out of line with many of the reported sayings of Jesus. To take but one example, the logic of the Lord's prayer – 'Forgive us our trespasses as we forgive those who trespass against us', together with its accompanying teaching – clearly implies that divine forgiveness is conditional on our own readiness to forgive: 'if you do not forgive others their sins, your Father will not forgive you your sins'.[28] To airbrush the sternness and severity of God out of the picture is to remove an element that is crucial to a proper understanding of religious awe, as we shall see in a moment.

But firstly, how are we to evaluate the main claim under discussion (one that finds increasing support in today's naturalistic climate) that it is quite possible to cultivate spiritual awareness without religion, in particular without theistic religion? It all depends on exactly what kind of awareness we are thinking of. It's a welcome development to find secularists such as Harris paying attention to the phenomenon of spiritual experience (the 'great hole in secularism, humanism, rationalism, atheism …'),[29] and acknowledging that there is more to understanding reality than many scientistically oriented philosophers are commonly prepared to allow. But spiritual experience cannot be considered in isolation, as a kind of 'self-standing' phenomenon, as it were. We always need to ask about what the experience is an experience *of*. And it is significant that the reality that is disclosed by spiritual experience according to Harris (strongly influenced here by Buddhism and kindred creeds) is a wholly impersonal one. It is not one that addresses us personally with a call to change, or requires anything of us, but is a blank and impersonal flux.

---

[28] Matthew 6:15; Mark 11:26. Compare May, *Love*, ch. 7: 'Why Christian love isn't unconditional'.

[29] Harris, *Waking Up*, p. 202.

Even the individual self – the sense of ourselves as unified subjects who are the 'experiencers of experience' – is, according to this impersonal picture of reality, an illusion.[30] Yet although the supposed non-existence of the self is presented as supported by scientific evidence about the workings of the brain, the empirical evidence in fact falls far short of the proposed conclusion. It is true that experiments with split-brain patients reveal much about the modular functioning of the mind, divided into relatively autonomous subsystems, and it is also true (as indeed has been clear since Freud) that our conscious thoughts reveal only a small fraction of what is going on in the mind; but none of this shows that it is a philosophical or scientific mistake for you or me to think of ourselves as genuine and unique subjects of experience enduring through time. Indeed, the personal narrative Harris himself provides in the course of the book about his own early life, and how his distinctive philosophical and spiritual outlook matured though the years, seems at every point implicitly to run counter to the official 'no-self' view he proclaims.

As for the techniques of spiritual mindfulness that are proposed, one may grant that these can indeed be cultivated in various ways, which do not require subscribing to any of the (supposedly suspect) theistic doctrines that are deplored. And many of the resulting states mentioned by Harris, and familiar from many types of Eastern religion, turn out to have very considerable appeal: a sense of 'selfless wellbeing', 'self-transcendence', 'paying attention to the present moment', a feeling of 'boundless love' (albeit of a fundamentally impersonal kind), a sense of being 'at one with the cosmos', and 'bringing stress to an end'.[31] Nothing I have so far said or will say is intended to deny the value of such goals. But for the purposes of the present argument, the point I wish to bring out is that they have very little in common with the religious encounters

---

[30] Harris, *Waking Up*, pp. 205–6.
[31] *Waking Up*, pp. 17, 18, 3, 5, 43, 48.

with the sacred explored in the previous section, those intensely *personal* encounters, infused with awe and charged with moral significance, where the individual feels him or herself to be checked, to be scrutinized, and to be called upon to respond and to change.

Set against this, the meditative goals of impersonal and boundless oceanic wellbeing have an essentially quietist character. They stem from a long Eastern tradition of spirituality in which the paramount objective is achieving bliss by detaching oneself from the stressful world of struggle, commitment and dependency. It is of course true that many Eastern sages advocate a path of virtue and right conduct (and indeed the compassionate outlook of many practitioners of Eastern spirituality is greatly to be respected and admired), so in this sense there is an ethical component involved. But it is not a component that is intrinsically connected to the underlying vision of the cosmos, for the Eastern vision is one in which personal commitments and demands are based on an illusion, and ultimate reality is simply an impersonal continuum of conditions that arise and pass away.

There is a fundamental contrast here with the kind of sacred vision recorded by Isaiah, where the seraphim cry 'Holy!' and the Temple shakes and is filled with smoke. The vision is one of surpassing beauty: a throne, high and lifted up, the angels, each with six wings, and the earth and heaven said to be filled with God's glory (*kavod*).[32] But the immediate reaction of the prophet who witnesses this vision is to cry 'Woe is me!' The vision is one in which there is that powerful intermingling of the aesthetic and the moral, of beauty and goodness, which we remarked on earlier as characteristic of the authentic encounter with the sacred. Isaiah, confronted with this mystery of perfection, acutely feels his own inadequacy, his own shortcomings and those of his people, and, in the ensuing story, is immediately called to action, to set about righting what is amiss.

---

[32] Isaiah 6:1–4. For the term 'glory' (*kavod*), see section 2, above.

All this is worlds away from the idea that focusing our attention on the present moment, or the merging of the self in an oceanic cosmos, is the key to spiritual health. On the contrary, we have a *demanding* vision, harshly out of key with the prevailing modern desire to be told that we all are fundamentally 'ok'. It is a vision that makes no sense without the two poles of the human condition that Blaise Pascal underlined – our wretchedness, or sinfulness, and our redeemability would we but turn towards the good.[33]

Sinfulness is of course another idea that consorts ill with modern secularist philosophy – indeed, a colleague fairly representative of today's prevailing anglophone philosophical naturalism once told me, with obviously genuine puzzlement, that among the many aspects of the religious outlook that baffled him was the concept of sin. Yet if we are prepared to set aside crude literalist interpretations of the garden of Eden story, and various convoluted theological formulations about the descendants of Adam and Eve being punished for their parents' transgressions, the basic idea of original sin incorporates a simple and undeniable truth – that we are a deeply flawed species, always ready to talk ourselves out of pursuing the good that is staring us in the face, and to turn away towards the specious but alluring prizes of quick gratification, power, control and self-aggrandizement. And once we *have* turned away, an abyss of evil is potentially ready to open before us, as the horrendous history of war and violence in our all-too-recent past should be more than enough to demonstrate.

It should now start to become clear that the sense of awe, which we have described as inextricably linked to an encounter with the sacred, cannot properly be reduced to an abject feeling of fear before an authority who will 'punish anyone who harbours the slightest doubt about his supremacy'. It is true that a certain kind of

---

[33] *Misère de l'homme sans Dieu ... Félicité de l'homme avec Dieu.* Blaise Pascal, *Pensées* [1670], ed. L. Lafuma (Paris: Seuil, 1962), no. 6.

fearful wonder is indeed involved, as in the famous saying 'the fear of the Lord is the beginning of wisdom';[34] but wisdom is not a cowed and cringing obedience simply to avoid punishment, but rather a true *understanding* of where our highest good lies. If, *per impossibile*, God were not good, says Thomas Aquinas, there would be no reason to love him.[35] God, and the ethical demand that flows from him, is inseparable from his goodness.[36]

But the theistic tradition reminds us that this highest good is nonetheless fearful, because it demands our giving up easier sources of gratification, and that sometimes the only way for that to happen is for us to be firmly checked and shaken out of our complacency. So once again we see that the opposition, so often highlighted by contemporary secularists, between the supposedly irrational metaphysical dogmas of religion and an enlightened morality of human values is based on a false contrast. For what the theistic tradition, properly understood, captures is the inexorable power and beauty of goodness, manifested in a specially vivid way in those experiences that we group under the heading of the sacred, where the fearfulness and the demandingness of this goodness is something that our own deepest human intuitions make it very difficult for us with integrity to deny.

4. The fires of arrogance

In that masterpiece composed at the close of the twentieth century, W. G. Sebald's *The Rings of Saturn*, the writer expresses, as so often in his work, a powerful sense of the erosion of meaning in life. The protagonist of the novel, walking along now largely deserted

---

[34] Proverbs 9:10; Psalms 111[110]:10.

[35] 'Dato, per impossibile, quod Deus non esset hominis bonum, non esset ei ratio diligendi.' Aquinas, *Summa theologiae* [1266–73], Part II, Second Part, Qu. 26, art. 13, ad 3.

[36] Compare Thomas Aquinas, *Compendium theologiae* [1273], Part I, ch. 109.

stretches of the coastal landscape of East Anglia, looks back to earlier medieval and Roman times when it was dotted by a series of bustling ports, and back millennia earlier, to a time when the land of Britain was almost entirely thickly wooded. He sees the history of humankind as that of a greedy and destructive species that continues to survive by quite literally burning everything in its path:

> Whatever was spared by the flames in prehistoric Europe was later felled for construction and shipbuilding, and to make the charcoal which the smelting of iron required in vast quantities. By the seventeenth century, only a few insignificant remnants of the erstwhile forests survived in the islands, most of them untended and decaying. The great fires were now lit on the other side of the ocean ... Our spread over the earth was fuelled by ... incessantly burning whatever would burn ... From the earliest times, human civilization has been no more than a strange luminescence growing more intense by the hour, of which no one can say when it will begin to wane and when it will fade away.[37]

The passage speaks of the arrogance of humanity, our relentless desire to impose our stamp on the world, even at the cost of destroying the very environment that sustains us. But more than that, it seems to hint at an underlying malaise, a futility. The 'strange luminescence' that is *homo sapiens* spreads like a rot over the planet, or like a heap of ants devouring a pile of sugar, until the resources are all consumed and it subsides and fades away.

Perhaps it is the inevitable fate of any successful biological species to multiply and to consume until it dooms itself to

---

[37] W. G. Sebald, *The Rings of Saturn* [*Die Ringe des Saturn*, 1995], trans. Michael Hulse (London: Random House, 2002), p. 170.

extinction unless externally curbed or checked. But here appears the further arrogance of humankind, which is of a different order from mere biological acquisitiveness: we imagine we are so totally in control, such grand 'autonomous agents', that we can shape the future as we see fit. This is both a blessing and a curse. It is a genuine and wonderful privilege of human beings that we are not just biologically determined creatures constrained by the conditions around us (though of course we are partly that), but have, uniquely, the power to see how things might be different, and the ability to deliberate so as to assess and evaluate which of the various possibilities before us should be actualized to further our needs and desires. But the concomitant risk is that we delude ourselves into supposing we have a more radical kind of autonomy: that we are somehow lords of existence with the power to create value by our own acts of will. This is the dangerous vision that inspired Friedrich Nietzsche when he heralded the emergence of a new type of human who would 'grow to such height and force as to feel the compulsion for a revaluation of values'.[38]

We need encounters with the sacred in order to douse such arrogance, to tame what Wordsworth called the 'pride of intellect and virtue's self-esteem'.[39] Encounters with the sacred tell us that we are not, and cannot be, creators of value: we can only *respond* to value. It may at first seem that we are able to create value, since it's clearly true that we have the power, the wonderful power, in our actions and in our artistic and cultural endeavours, to produce things that are beautiful and good. But in doing this we are not creating beauty and goodness, we are simply *transmitting* or *channelling* them.

---

[38] Friedrich Nietzsche, *Beyond Good and Evil* [*Jenseits von Gut und Böse*, 1886], §203.

[39] William Wordsworth, *The Prelude*, Bk II (1850 version), ed. J. C. Maxwell (Harmondsworth: Penguin, 1988).

Some may dispute this: are not terms like 'beautiful' and 'good' just labels for what we through our human conventions decide to approve of? To use the immortal phrase of Evelyn Waugh, 'up to a point, Lord Copper'[40] – or, in plain English, no. It is true that much in the world of the arts depends on human attitudes and conventions and the boundaries of what counts as a 'work of art' are, as we all know, constantly being challenged, sometimes in ways that have the beneficial function of shaking us out of our complacency and entrenched habits of response. But none of this really erodes the status of beauty as a genuine and objective value, a value which it is not simply up to us to define and determine. Different cultures, to be sure, have different conceptions of what is aesthetically pleasing, but in each case the evaluations in question must be based not on arbitrary choice or subjective decision but on objective features – patterns of colour and form, resonances of harmony, rhythm or melody, configurations of word and meaning, that speak to the human condition and make for beauty.

And so for goodness. Just as with the beauties of nature and of great works of art, so with right action, and the long list of fine and admirable deeds famously catalogued by St Paul: 'whatsoever things are true, whatsoever things are honest, whatsoever things are just, whatsoever things are pure, whatsoever things are lovely, whatsoever things are of good report'.[41] Such actions have the power to 'lift us up when fallen',[42] or, in the striking words of Hopkins, 'they rain upon our much thick and marsh air/ rich beams …'.[43] – in other words, they illuminate what would otherwise be the murky drudgery and moral dinginess of our lives with something objectively precious, something in virtue of which life is after all meaningful and good.

---

[40] Evelyn Waugh, *Scoop* [1938] (London: Penguin, 2000).

[41] Philippians 4:8.

[42] Wordsworth, *The Prelude* (1850), Book II, lines 21–2.

[43] G. M. Hopkins, 'The Lantern out of Doors' (1877).

In our present-day Western philosophical culture, there are very large numbers (including, perhaps surprisingly, the majority of those philosophers who have rejected theism) who still harbour a powerful wish that our human lives should not be determined by mere subjective desire or preference, but be directed towards real, objective value. Despite the rise of secularism, people find it very hard to give up the view that there are, in the words of the brilliant and highly respected British philosopher Derek Parfit, 'irreducibly normative truths'[44] – in other words, that there are moral truths, not reducible to factual truths about the natural world, which have objective authority over us, and which require us to act in certain ways. But it is not easy to combine this view with the prevailing naturalistic conception of the world (also espoused by Parfit) in which there are no 'strange' parts of reality – in which there is no transcendent source of value, and where the only ultimate constituents of the world are the physical objects studied by science. Faced with this impasse, many other contemporary philosophers have been tempted to try to reduce the source of meaning and value to a mere function of our own chosen 'projects' or our own 'self-constitution'.[45]

But our own self-conception proves, in the end, an unstable and uncertain signpost to meaning and value. To borrow an image from G. K. Chesterton, 'what we all dread is a maze with no centre, and that is why atheism is a nightmare'.[46] If we have at the centre of our lives no more than our own projects or self-image to guide us, there will be no ultimate objective grounding to our being in the world – nothing beyond our own finite and contingent selves

---

[44] Derek Parfit, *On What Matters* (Oxford: Oxford University Press, 2011), Part II, p. 464.

[45] See Bernard Williams, *Shame and Necessity* (Berkeley: University of California Press, 1993); Christine Korsgaard, *The Sources of Normativity* (Cambridge: Cambridge University Press, 1996).

[46] G. K. Chesterton, 'Caesar's Head', from *The Wisdom of Father Brown* [1914].

to serve as an orientation for our lives. That nightmare could, of course, be the truth – it cannot be logically disproved. But our encounters with the sacred seem to tell us that there *is* a centre to the confusing maze that is the human condition, and that at that centre lies objective beauty and goodness.

Yet the believer always needs to remember that faith in such ultimate objectivity can never license the arrogant assumption that we have a privileged hotline to the truth. The glimpses afforded by what we call experiences of the sacred do not provide a guaranteed map through to the centre, or a verifiable proof of what lies there. On the contrary, the best we can have is a sense of awe at something we aspire to, but of which we fall far short, and an all-too-clear recognition that the pathway cannot be certified in advance. But the 'rich beams' that we glimpse through our 'much thick and marsh air' give us hope that even though there may be many false steps ahead, and many wrong pathways, the journey is one that ultimately makes sense.

Chapter 6

Something of Great Constancy

Yet all the story of the night told o'er
And all their minds transfigured so together
More witnesseth than fancy's images
And grows to something of great constancy,
But howsoever, strange and admirable.

Shakespeare[1]

1. From fancy to reality

At the start of the final act of *A Midsummer Night's Dream*, Duke Theseus, the archetypal hard-nosed rationalist, expresses his scepticism about the stories the two pairs of young lovers have related about their magical night in the forest, and the strange transformation in their relations to each other – a transformation perhaps best expressed by the previously sullen and moping Helena when, on waking up, she joyfully tells the Duke: 'And I have found Demetrius like a jewel, mine own and not mine own.'[2] Theseus later confides to his own bride Hippolyta that he can never believe this sort of stuff: the wild imaginings of the lover are like

---

[1] William Shakespeare, *A Midsummer Night's Dream* [c.1595], Act V, scene 1.

[2] Ibid., Act IV, scene 1. In Benjamin Britten's operatic version of the play, the lines are turned into a mysteriously beautiful quartet (a rendition may be heard at https://www.youtube.com/watch?v=KFhXWrXLQ6U, accessed 31 January 2015).

the rantings of the lunatic or the poet, making a fuss about what is in reality 'airy nothing'.

But Hippolyta, in the lines from our epigraph, begs to differ. Yes, the story may be 'strange' and 'admirable' (to be wondered at), but for all that, the fact that all four lovers have undergone such a transformation, their minds 'transfigured together', points to something more than just the images of fantasy (or 'fancy'). It 'grows' to something of 'great constancy': there is a kind of internal consistency or coherence about it that cannot so easily be set aside.

Theseus, of course, will not be convinced. His down-to-earth, common-sense world, which dismisses whatever cannot be empirically verified as 'airy nothing', is forearmed against refutation. And yet the audience, if the play has been well done, will all be on the side of Hippolyta. For in the mysterious wood outside Athens, where the practical concerns of everyday life are set aside, they have indeed seen strange and 'admirable' events taking place, events which seem to show there is more to reality than what can be catalogued in terms of plain unvarnished fact.

It is unhelpful to suppose that this 'more', this extra dimension of reality, can best be explicated in terms of the operation of occult supernatural powers and forces – as if the truth of what is told in this play hinges on whether the existence of fairies can be verified. To look at it this way makes it seem as if the validity of the narrative depends on the kind of nonsense investigated by so-called 'spiritualists' in the early decades of the twentieth century, as in the photographical plates of the 'Cottingley fairies' that Sir Arthur Conan Doyle became for a time very enthusiastic about as evidence of 'psychic phenomena'.[3] But Shakespeare's Oberon and Titania and their fairy attendants are not portrayed as weird 'spooky' entities, but are closely associated with the blessings and

---

[3] See Arthur Conan Doyle, *The Coming of the Fairies* (1922). It emerged many decades later that the photographs had been faked.

beauties of the natural world, with the 'fair blessed beams' of the rising sun that turns the salt waves of the sea into 'yellow gold';[4] they are powers who 'make sport with the morning's love', and who close the play by blessing the pairs of newly wedded lovers. To be sure, they are spirits of the night, beyond the threshold of sober mundane scrutiny of the kind championed by Theseus, so in this sense they cannot be detected in a scientific inventory of the 'natural world'. But their presence in the world is nevertheless manifest, like the 'blessing in this gentle breeze' that Wordsworth joyfully acclaims;[5] for in virtue of the power that they represent, reality is disclosed as irradiated with meaning, and ultimately with goodness. Transcendence and immanence here fuse, for the world turns out to be *deep*, 'deeper than day can comprehend',[6] a world where the quarrels and bickering and jealousies of our competitive biological nature can be redeemed and transformed by a love that is found 'like a jewel, mine own and not mine own'.

Keeping this kind of example in mind may perhaps give us some hints as to how a religious and in particular theistic conception of reality should best be understood. The religious vision, or so we have in effect been suggesting throughout the book, is one that accords with some of the most significant and resonant aspects of our human experience, and once we are prepared to entertain and embrace it, it coheres, and 'grows to something of great constancy'. None of this is to say that those who take the side represented by Theseus can be proved wrong. The scientistic, the rationalistic, the atheistic view of things is not incoherent, and it is no part of our

---

[4] Shakespeare, *A Midsummer Night's Dream*, Act III, scene 2. I am grateful to Roger Warren for drawing my attention, many years ago, to the importance of such passages.

[5] William Wordsworth, *The Prelude* [1805/1850], opening line.

[6] *Die Welt ist tief/Und tiefer as der Tag gedacht* ('the world is deep, and deeper that the day had thought'); Friedrich Nietzsche, 'O Mensch! Gib acht', from *Also Sprach Zarathustra* [1884], Part III.

purpose in charting the path towards belief to impugn the sincerity or the logic of those who are averse to following that path. The argument of this book has not been intended to be coercive, nor could it be; it aims, rather, to provide a field of reference within which religious belief can orient itself – a 'system of co-ordinates', rooted in the culture that has so long sustained us, within which our deepest intuitions of value and meaning make sense.

2. The costs of belief

Coherent or not, it is plain that the religious framework is one that many in our contemporary culture are fully prepared to jettison. Many have already done so without apparent loss of purpose and equilibrium, and it would be absurd to suggest that a 'life after faith' (or indeed a life where faith has never taken root in the first place) cannot be a valuable and worthwhile one; it is still more absurd to suggest that it cannot be a morally good one, or an aesthetically and emotionally satisfying one. So we come full circle back to the 'contrasting visions' explored in our opening chapter. In an ambiguous world, where conflicting interpretations of the reality we inhabit appear to be capable of being espoused by equally reflective and sincere thinkers, is there any decisive reason to take the path of belief rather than its opposite?

If 'decisive' means unambiguously supported by empirical evidence, or demonstrable by logically watertight reasoning, then the answer, confirmed by the overwhelming philosophical consensus from the past few hundred years, must be no. But suppose that someone is, in spite of that, drawn to the kinds of consideration we have been exploring in earlier chapters. Suppose that person does feel the yearning for 'ontological rootedness', for being able to feel his or her existence is grounded in an objective source of meaning and value. And suppose they recognize in their lives that there have been moments of 'transcendence', sacred moments when the mundanities of ordinary life fall away and something is glimpsed which does not fit into the scientistic picture that tells us that the world of physics is all that there ultimately is. Are there, in such a case, considerations available that make it at least reasonable to choose the path of belief?

We are faced with a puzzle here, which, if it is to be solved at all, must partly be solved by action and commitment, for as with so many of the vital decisions of life, to remain detached until certified evidence presents itself can be a recipe for blunting the receptivity through which alone the requisite changes in sensibility might be forthcoming.[7] Yet taking the plunge and opening oneself to the possibility of a radical shift in one's worldview is liable to be inhibited by all sorts of influences, often operating at a pre-rational level. One of these is peer pressure; for although academics and scholars are prone to pride themselves on their splendid independence of mind, the subliminal pressure to conform to contemporary intellectual fashion may be much stronger than is often suspected. A colleague working in a literature department once told me that if it got around that she was spending time in her lectures discussing religious interpretations of poetry, her academic reputation would be sure to suffer: such an approach simply did not fit in with the prevailing ethos of the department, or with the expectations of the most influential journal editors.

These matters of group and hierarchical pressure may vary from subject to subject, from institution to institution, and from country to country. Those working in North America, where there are many opportunities for academic advancement in the large number of respected institutions of tertiary education that have an explicitly religious ethos, may argue that so far from the cards being stacked against religious belief, there are many places where it gets a comparatively easy ride. But in many parts of the

---

[7] See Foreword, and Chapter 3, section 2, above.

anglophone academy, including some of the most prestigious and influential, the story is a different one. In general, there is clearly something that might be called a prevailing climate of ideas that pervades our intellectual culture and results in all sorts of ways in a negative or sceptical perception of religious belief in the modern Western academy.

The *phenomenon* of religion of course remains of powerful interest to contemporary historians and cultural commentators, particularly since the traumatic events of '9/11' and its aftermath, but that is a quite separate matter from the increasing disdain in our contemporary Western intellectual culture for concepts and ideas that presuppose the possible truth of religious belief as such. To give but one instance, the more terms like 'post-Christian' are used by sophisticated academics and essayists, then the more the subtle subconscious peer pressure grows to be in tune with the 'intellectual climate of the times'. There are of course many who succeed in bucking the trend, but this is not easy, particularly for those starting out on their careers, since one's status as a writer and a thinker, the likelihood of being invited to cultural events and discussion panels, and a host of other small but important influences (patterns of conversation, sense of humour, the whole network of professional camaraderie) all hinge on an implicitly presupposed accord about the future shape of our intellectual dialogue in which theistic belief in general, and Christianity in particular, are assumed to have an increasingly marginal role.

Such influences also operate at earlier stages of life, as can be seen in Britain in the gradual change from an educational world in which every schoolchild was expected to have lessons on 'Scripture' (that is, the Bible), to one where this was replaced by something rather less clearly specified, namely 'RE', or 'religious education', which in turn gave way to the present-day emphasis on 'comparative religion'. The point of referring to this shift is not to disparage the comparative study of religion (which can no doubt bring many benefits), but to draw attention to the effects of the shift on the complex inherited background of ideas against which we all learn to shape our understanding of the world. It's hard to deny that the teaching of Scripture, whatever its merits or defects, and whatever one's particular attitude to Christianity, served the function of transmitting a culture – the culture that deeply informed so much Western art and music and literature and philosophy for so many centuries – and provided at least some degree of acquaintance with its founding narratives. By contrast, the move towards replacing this with a survey of a wide spectrum of beliefs and faiths inevitably removes them to a certain distance, as objects of detached scrutiny, to be inspected (often cursorily, given the size of the spectrum and the time available) rather as a visiting anthropologist might, and without any opportunity for deeper engagement with the texts (whether from a moral, or literary or philosophical perspective). Studying religion as a menagerie of weird and conflicting beliefs, known about only in outline, is very different from learning about it as part of the structural background of one's culture and civilization. There are, at the very least, interesting questions to be asked here about the effects of all this, at both the rational and the pre-rational level, on the sensibilities of each new generation.

These are perhaps issues for sociologists and psychologists to examine rather than matters which contribute directly to the religious and philosophical inquiry undertaken in these pages. But it is nonetheless important to be aware that in our inquiry about the path towards (or away from) religious belief we are not dealing with a timeless decision taken in some antechamber or 'green room', away from the complex social setting in which our lives have to be conducted. The question at stake for someone contemplating becoming, or ceasing to become, a believer, or returning to a previously abandoned faith, is not just about giving or withholding assent to some set of propositions or claims, nor even about subscribing to a certain outlook. It is about my whole identity – how I perceive myself, and how others perceive me. Religious belief determines where we are located in the world and in relation to others and it touches our most profound sense of who and what we are. Becoming or not becoming a believer, in short, is a matter that determines the shape and meaning of our lives as little else can do, and given all the social influences that confront us, some clearly apparent, some exerting subtle and barely perceivable pressures, the choices involved are ones that tax our self-awareness and our integrity to the limit.

3. Embodied engagement

The issues broached in the previous section serve to remind us that 'believing' is a far deeper and more complex phenomenon than is often assumed by those philosophers who are preoccupied with the epistemic status of our beliefs – that is, with how far our beliefs are warranted, what evidence supports them, and whether or not they are entitled to the accolade 'knowledge'. All those philosophical questions, important though they are, tend to presuppose that belief is a relatively 'transparent' phenomenon, something about how the mind's stock of conscious ideas is ordered so as to conform to certain rational patterns of justification. Few philosophers nowadays are 'dualists' (that is, few still regard the mind as an immaterial substance), but for all that many still tend to think of the human mind as a kind of abstract intellect, where the inputs can in principle be expressed as transparent propositions or truths, and the outputs (if the system is working properly) are the resulting rationally appropriate beliefs.

But we are not abstract intellects, we are not even 'minds': we are creatures of flesh and blood, and when we speak of our 'minds', this is a way of referring to a complicated network of dispositions and processes and functions that are inextricably bound up with the workings of our bodies and our brains, evolved over countless millennia, and further moulded by a long and complex nexus of social and cultural pressures. Belief, in short, has an 'archaeology', as the theologian Graham Ward has put it: it is shaped by our primordial history in ways our conscious reflective minds are often only minimally aware of. Our desires and hopes and attitudes, the way we believe and think and act, are all mediated by 'symbolic realms that we, as hominid and human creatures, have been cultivating for 2.2 million years'.[8]

So there is layer upon layer of belief formation and belief shaping. We do not just take in evidence and form hypotheses – we anticipate, we project, we hope, we fear, we recognize, we remember, we associate, and we constantly communicate and interact with others. And all this we do as embodied, biological organisms, and in virtue of the workings of our brains, which are themselves, as we now know, modular – made up of partly autonomous but constantly interacting neurological subsystems which enable us to have different modes of awareness of the world. This brings us back to the groundbreaking work of Iain McGilchrist, to which we alluded at the very start of this book.[9] For although the precise details of his account of the functions of the left and right hemispheres of the brain have been much debated, his fundamental thesis is hard to deny: that in addition to the faculties typically associated with the left brain, whereby we analyse, classify and dissect in a detached and abstract manner, there are those more intuitive 'right brain' modes of awareness, often emotionally or 'affectively' toned, whereby we grasp reality in ways that are far more direct and engaged than happens with the deliverances of rational deliberation.

---

[8] Graham Ward, *Unbelievable* (New York: I.B. Tauris, 2014), p. 181.
[9] Iain McGilchrist, *The Master and his Emissary* (New Haven: Yale University Press, 2009); see Foreword, p. x, above.

But we need both modes of understanding if we are to flourish as human beings. And this connects crucially with the question that has been preoccupying us in one way or another throughout this book, the question of how we are to arrive at a worldview that answers to our human needs and does justice to the full range of our human experience of the world. In this search, we need *all* the resources of the human mind – not just the analytic intellect, but the totality of what is revealed by our imaginative, affective and creative engagement with the reality around us.[10]

This may perhaps go some way to explaining the strategy adopted throughout these pages, namely that of interleaving the formal argumentation at many points with discussion of literary and artistic and scriptural sources. These are not just 'examples' or illustrations, tacked on as embellishments to the serious business of argument; nor are they (as the followers of Duke Theseus are likely to complain) rhetorical devices designed to cloud the mind or paper over gaps in the evidence. On the contrary, they are an indispensible and integral part of the philosophical enterprise in hand: the struggle to grasp the nature and significance of belief in general and religious belief in particular, and to understand how such belief can earn our allegiance, and be embraced as reasonable, coherent and properly grounded in how we experience the world.

In our contemporary philosophical culture, religion is classified by many as obsolete mythmaking, soon to be swept away by the continued march of science. We are surely right to hope that science will march forward to ever more powerful and compelling explanations of the phenomena around us, for modern science is among our greatest human achievements, and our debt to it is incalculable. What is wrong is the upholding of scientific

---

[10] For more on this, see Mark Wynn, *Emotional Experience and Religious Understanding: Integrating Perception, Conception and Feeling* (Cambridge: Cambridge University Press, 2005).

discourse as a template for all valid human understanding. Many of our most profound and illuminating modes of apprehending the reality in which we live do not and cannot depend on the formulation of abstract explanatory hypotheses, or the working out of mathematical or mechanical models, but require instead a kind of creative engagement with the world, which, in the end, is inseparable from any worthwhile human endeavour – including of course the scientific endeavour itself.

Some of that creative engagement we may call 'mythmaking'. But the typical modern associations of that word, classifying it simply as fiction, are rather like the associations that lead Duke Theseus to dismiss imagination as mere 'fantasy' or 'fancy', conjuring up 'airy nothings'. Yet the 'symbolic realms' we humans have cultivated for millions of years are, as Graham Ward reminds us, not mere fictional inventions, but embrace a rich array of cognitive and affective and practical modes of expression, including painting and poetry, music and ritual. In ways we cannot fully understand, these interlocking modes of human culture tap the powers of what for want of a better term we call the imagination, which operates at many more levels than are accessed by our conscious reflective awareness. Such works 'intimate that our experience ... of being in the world is freighted with a significance that only an appeal to the mythic can index'.[11]

None of this means we should go too far down the 'postmodernist' path, or wholly elide the distinction between *mythos* and *logos*, inventive dreaming and clear rationality. For the case put forward here is most emphatically *not* a matter of downgrading logic or of exalting irrationality. It is, on the contrary, a calm and sober recognition of our status as embodied beings who can only understand reality by engaging with it, and who can only properly engage with it by deploying *all* the faculties and modes of

---

[11] Ward, *Unbelievable*, pp. 185–6.

awareness that have enabled our species to survive and flourish in the world. It is through our multi-faceted embodied engagement with the world that we open ourselves to ever more dimensions of our existence and allow ourselves to become what we are meant to be – the species with the unique power to discern the meaning and the value of the reality that surrounds us.

4. What are days for?

'What are days for?' asks Philip Larkin in one of his more chilling poems. He answers:

> Days are where we live.
> They come, they wake us
> Time and time over.
> They are to be happy in:
> Where can we live but days?[12]

Such a seemingly bland and simple question. But behind it lies the horror and fear that is characteristically present in so much of Larkin's writing. For the poem will end by telling us that the real answer to the question of what days are for will 'bring the priest and the doctor / in their long coats / running over the fields'. In Larkin's fearful vision of the world, life is a bleakly repeated series of awakenings, morning after morning, offering a slim chance, all too often missed, to grab what happiness we may before the ultimate futility of extinction. It is true that Larkin's most often quoted line, from the conclusion of another poem, seems to speak of something of more enduring value – 'What will survive of us is

---

[12] Philip Larkin, 'Days' [1953], published in *The Whitsun Weddings* (1964). A reading of the poem by the author is available at https://www.youtube.com/watch?v=psyNfHyK17A (accessed 15 April 2015).

love'.[13] But the rest of that poem (about the medieval stone effigies of the Earl and Countess of Arundel) gives the lie to the idealistic sentiment – indeed the poem's final verdict is that the sentiment is at best 'almost true'. The couple's 'supine stationary voyage' down the centuries, as time slowly erodes the inscriptions round the tomb and successive generations of tourists come to gawp at them locked together, bears witness to a 'stone fidelity they never meant'.

Larkin's voice is in many ways the authentic voice of modernity, wistfully half-idealistic, but with a sour underlying tone of disappointed cynicism, ultimately self-absorbed and bleakly realistic (in its own eyes at least) about the truth of a world where there is no ultimate and reliable foothold for meaning and value outside of our own human finitude and our inadequate, conflicted and unsatisfactory bundle of wants and needs. It is, of course, a possible vision to hold – and the resonance of Larkin's poetic voice bears witness to the fact that it can find eloquent expression. But to revert to the question posed in our opening chapter,[14] is it really a vision that anyone could sincerely wish to embrace, given the option of something more sustaining, more energizing, more uplifting, and more nurturing of our nobler drives towards commitment and hope?

The answer to the last question is clear enough: all of us would, other things being equal, prefer something better. We would prefer to have that indefinable sense of grounding, to be able somehow to trust, with Tennyson, 'in the deep night, that all is well'.[15] What is perhaps still not finally clear, even after retracing all the steps we have taken in this book, is how to get to that destination – *how to believe*. And there may in the end be no

---

[13] Philip Larkin, 'An Arundel Tomb' [1956], from *The Whitsun Weddings*.

[14] See Chapter 1, sections 1 and 2, above.

[15] Alfred Tennyson, *In Memoriam* (1849), stanza CXXVI.

general and definitive answer to that question. The solution may ultimately depend on each individual's life and background and circumstances. So let us close instead, as we did at the end of the first instalment of this diptych (the companion volume *Why Believe?*), by picking out one among many revealing instances from the work of one of the world's very greatest creative geniuses, himself an exemplar of unfailing faith.

The early Bach cantata *Aus der Tiefen rufe ich, Herr, zu dir* ('Out of the deep I call to you, O Lord') (BWV 131) is a setting of the penitential Psalm *De Profundis*, (Psalm 130 [129]), first performed at Mühlhausen in 1708, when Bach was twenty-two, and very possibly commissioned in the wake of a devastating fire in town where many had lost their lives. The fourth section of the cantata sets the sixth verse of the Psalm, *meine Seele wartet auf den Herrn von einer Morgenwache bis zu der andern* ('my soul waits for the Lord, from one morning watch to the next'), and is scored for tenor solo with cello and organ continuo, the tenor melody being interleaved with an alto chorale to the words of a verse of a late sixteenth-century hymn which speaks of a longing for healing and redemption.[16]

Some commentators have criticized the music as 'repetitious', but the almost obsessive repeating of the phrase *meine Seele wartet* ('my soul waits') is surely the whole point of the aria, and a sign of Bach's consummate artistry. The tenor line deliberately emphasizes the almost unbearably protracted term of the expectant longing, the voice rising again and again and again with a plaintive melisma on the first syllable of the word *wartet* ('waits'); in the climax of the aria the stretching out of the longing, day after day, is further underlined in the phrase 'from one morning watch to the next'. And yet strangely, and this is the wonderful faith that informs

---

[16] A performance of the aria conducted by Ton Koopman with the Amsterdam Baroque Orchestra and Chorus may be heard at https://www.youtube.com/watch?v=cU-xnyHWy2U (accessed 15 April 2015).

Bach's genius, the music does not express a whining or a cringing or a peremptory or a flagging or an exhausted demand, but instead the sinuous 12/8 rhythm captures a steady pulse of hope, a calm flowing determination to open one's heart in the midst of need.

There is no rigid dogma here, no doctrinal inflexibility, no demand for the expulsion of the unbeliever, no sneering critical voice triumphantly pointing out that faith is absurd since the various religions and denominations all contradict one another. There is only what is universal to the human condition – the lonely voice of the human soul, crying out in direst need, calling to God because there is nowhere else to go, because the voice can and must be heard. And there is no simple answer given, no magical solution, but the voice goes on calling, day after day, from one morning watch to the next. And as the uplifting melodic line gives voice to this longing, we suddenly know the answer to Larkin's bleak and frightening question – we know 'what days are for'. They are not for 'being happy in', as Larkin self-pityingly and querulously demands they should be (though of course we all want happiness); they are not for self-importantly pursuing our 'projects', which we arrogantly declare can be the source of value and meaning (though to be sure we are required to set ourselves worthwhile objectives in life). The days that have been given us are for learning, for hoping, for growing, for waiting, for turning towards the good even in the depth of sorrow, for lifting up the heart in expectation and in love.

This surely is what Ludwig Wittgenstein meant when he said that 'someone to whom it is given in ultimate distress to open his heart instead of contracting it absorbs the remedy into his heart'.[17] There is no better expression of what the religious outlook is about, and although Wittgenstein himself declined to be classified as 'religious', the insight into the psychology of the

---

[17] Ludwig Wittgenstein, MS of 1944, in *Culture and Value*, ed. Georg Henrik Wright, Heikki Nyman and Alois Pichler (Oxford: Blackwell, 1980), pp. 52–3.

believer that he displays here carries an implicit conviction that what is going on is not delusion or wishful thinking or neurotic anxiety or superstitious irrationality, but 'something of great constancy'. All that is needed is an openness of heart in order for the remedy, available to all, to be received for what it is: a true and precious gift.

Bibliography

Aquinas, Thomas, *Summa theologiae* [1266–73], trans. Fathers of the English Dominican Province (London: Burns, Oates & Washbourne, 1911).

Benson, H. et al., 'Study of the Therapeutic Effects of Intercessory Prayer (STEP)', *American Heart Journal* 151–4 (2006), 934–42.

Bergson, Henri, *The Creative Mind* [*La Pensée et le mouvant*, 1933], trans. Mabelle L. Andison (New York: The Wisdom Library, 1946).

Betjeman, John, *A Few Late Chrysanthemums* (London: Murray, 1954).

Botton, Alain de and Armstrong, John, *Art as Therapy* (London: Phaidon, 2013).

Burnshaw, Stanley, *The Poem Itself* (Harmondsworth: Penguin, 1960).

Carlisle, Clare, *On Habit* (London: Routledge, 2014).

Chappell, S. G. (ed.), *Intuition, Theory, and Anti-theory in Ethics* (Oxford: Oxford University Press, 2015).

Chesterton, G. K., *The Wisdom of Father Brown* [1914], in *The Penguin Complete Father Brown* (Harmondsworth: Penguin, 1981).

Clayton, P. and Peacocke, A. (eds), *In Whom We Live and Move and Have Our Being* (Grand Rapids, MI: Eerdmans, 2004).

Conrad, Joseph, *Letters to Cunninghame Graham*, ed. C. T. Watts (Cambridge: Cambridge University Press, 1969).

Cooper, David, *A Philosophy of Gardens* (Oxford: Clarendon Press, 2006).

Cottingham, J. (ed.), *Western Philosophy* (Oxford: Blackwell, 1996).

—— *Cartesian Reflections* (Oxford: Oxford University Press, 2008).

—— *Why Believe?* (London: Continuum, 2009).

—— 'Human Nature and the Transcendent', in Constantine Sandis and M. J. Cain (eds), *Human Nature*. Royal Institute of Philosophy supplement 70 (Cambridge: Cambridge University Press, 2012), pp. 233–54.

—— *Philosophy of Religion: Towards a More Humane Approach* (Cambridge: Cambridge University Press, 2014).

Dawkins, Richard, *Rivers Out of Eden* (New York: Basic Books, 1995).

—— *Unweaving the Rainbow* (London: Penguin, 1998).

Descartes, René, *Discourse on the Method* [*Discours de la méthode*, 1637]; *Meditations on First Philosophy* [*Meditationes de prima philosophia*, 1641]; *The Passions of the Soul* [*Les passions de l'âme*, 1649]; and Correspondence. All works of Descartes cited may be found in C. Adam and P. Tannery, *Œuvres de Descartes* (12 vols, revised edn, Paris: Vrin/CNRS, 1964–76) (known as 'AT'); English translation by J. Cottingham, R. Stoothoff and D. Murdoch, *The Philosophical Writings of Descartes* (2 vols, Cambridge: Cambridge University Press, 1985) (known as 'CSM'), and vol. III, *The Correspondence*, by the same translators and A. Kenny (Cambridge: Cambridge University Press, l991) (known as 'CSMK').

Donne, John, *The Works of John Donne*, ed. H. Alford (London: Parker, 1839).

Edwards, Jonathan, *A Treatise Concerning Religious Affections* (Philadelphia: Crissy, 1821).

Ellis, Fiona, *God, Value, and Nature* (Oxford: Oxford University Press, 2014).

Feltham, B. and Cottingham, J. (eds), *Partiality and Impartiality: Morality, Special Relationships, and the Wider World* (Oxford: Oxford University Press, 2010).

Girard, René, *Violence and the Sacred* [*La Violence et le sacré*, 1972] (London: Bloomsbury, 2013).

Godwin, William, *Enquiry Concerning Political Justice and its Influence on Modern Morals and Happiness* [1798], 3rd edn, ed. I. Kramnick (London: Penguin, 1985).

Hare, John, *The Moral Gap: Kantian Ethics, Human Limits and God's Assistance* (Oxford: Clarendon, 1996).

Harris, Sam, *The End of Faith* (New York: Norton, 2005).

—— *Waking Up: A Guide to Spirituality Without Religion* (New York: Simon & Schuster, 2014).

Heaney, Seamus, *Finders Keepers: Selected Prose 1971–2001* (London: Faber, 2002).

Heidegger, Martin, *Being and Time* [*Sein und Zeit*, 1927], trans. J. Macquarrie and E. Robinson (New York: Harper & Row, 1962).

Hick, John, *An Interpretation of Religion: Human Responses to the Transcendent* [1989], 2nd edn (Houndmills: Palgrave, 2004).

Hopkins, Gerard Manley, *Note-books and Papers*, ed. H. House
(Oxford: Oxford University Press, 1937).

—— *The Poems and Prose of Gerard Manley Hopkins*, ed. W. H.
Gardner (Harmondsworth: Penguin, 1953).

—— *The Major Works*, ed. C. Phillips (Oxford: Oxford University
Press, 2002).

Hume, David, *A Treatise of Human Nature* [1739–40], ed. D. F.
Norton and M. J. Norton (Oxford: Oxford University Press, 2000).

Husserl, Edmund, *Cartesian Meditations* [*Cartesianische Meditationen*,
1931], trans. D. Cairns (The Hague: Nijhoff, 1960).

Johnston, Mark, *Saving God: Religion after Idolatry* (Princeton, NJ:
Princeton University Press, 2009).

Kant, Immanuel, *Critique of Judgement* [*Kritik der Urteilskraft*, 1790],
trans. J. Meredith (Clarendon: Oxford, 1991).

—— *Prolegomena to any Future Metaphysic that will be able to
present itself as a Science* [*Prolegomena zu einer jeden künftigen
Metaphysik die als Wissenschaft wird auftreten können*, 1783], ed.
G. Zöller and P. Lucas (Oxford: Oxford University Press, 2004).

Korsgaard, Christine, *The Sources of Normativity* (Cambridge:
Cambridge University Press, 1996).

Lacewing, Michael, 'Can Non-theists Appropriately Feel Existential
Gratitude?', *Religious Studies*, 2015, available on CJO2015. DOI:
10.1017/S0034412515000037.

Larkin, Philip, *The Complete Poems* (London: Faber, 2012).

Leibniz, Gottfried Wilhelm, *Monadology* [*La Monadologie*, 1714],
trans. E. M. Huggard (London: Routledge, 1951).

Lingard, John, 'Kurt Wallander's Journey into Autumn', in
    Scandinavian-Canadian Studies 17 (2006–7), 104–5.

Løgstrup, Knud E., *The Ethical Demand* [*Den Etiske Fordring*, 1956],
    ed. H. Fink and A. MacIntyre (Notre Dame, IL: University of Notre
    Dame Press, 1997).

MacSwain, Robert, *Solved By Sacrifice: Austin Farrer, Fideism, and the
    Evidence of Faith* (Leuven: Peeters, 2013).

Mankell, Henning, *The Fifth Woman* [*Den femte kvinnan*, 1996], trans.
    Steven T. Murray (New York: Vintage Crime, 2004).

May, Simon, *Love: A History* (New Haven, CT: Yale University Press,
    2011).

McGhee, Michael, *Transformations of Mind* (Cambridge: Cambridge
    University Press, 2000).

McGilchrist, Iain, *The Master and his Emissary* (New Haven: Yale
    University Press, 2009).

Milton, John, *Paradise Lost* [1674], ed. H. Darbishire (London: Oxford
    University Press, 1958).

Moore, Adrian, *The Evolution of Modern Metaphysics: Making Sense of
    Things* (Cambridge: Cambridge University Press, 2012).

Moser, Paul, *The Elusive God: Reorienting Religious Epistemology*
    (Cambridge: Cambridge University Press, 2008).

Nietzsche, Friedrich, *Beyond Good and Evil* [*Jenseits von Gut und Böse*,
    1886], trans. W. Kaufmann (New York: Random House, 1966).

Parfit, Derek, *On What Matters* (Oxford: Oxford University Press,
    2011).

Pascal, Blaise, *Pensées* [*c*.1660], ed. L. Lafuma (Paris: Seuil, 1962).

Pullman, Philip, *The Amber Spyglass* (London: Fickling, 2000).

Putnam, Hilary, 'The Meaning of Meaning' [1975], in *Philosophical Papers*, vol. 2 (Cambridge: Cambridge University Press, 1985).

Russell, Bertrand, *The Collected Papers of Bertrand Russell*, vol. 11 (London: Routledge, 1977).

Scruton, Roger, *The Face of God* (London: Continuum, 2012).

Sebald, W. G., *The Rings of Saturn* [*Die Ringe des Saturn*, 1995], trans. Michael Hulse (London: Random House, 2002).

Shafer-Landau, Russ, 'Ethics as Philosophy: A Defense of Ethical Non-Naturalism', in *Metaethics After Moore*, ed. Mark Timmons and Terry Horgan (Oxford: Oxford University Press, 2006), pp. 209–33.

Shakespeare, William, *The Complete Works*, 2nd edn (Oxford: Clarendon, 2006).

Steiner, George, *Heidegger*, 2nd edn (London: Fontana, 1992).

Sylvester, Joshua, *A Garland of Christmas Carols, Ancient and Modern* (London: Hotten, 1861).

Taylor, Charles, *A Secular Age* (Cambridge, MA: Harvard University Press, 2007).

Tennyson, Alfred Lord, *In Memoriam* and 'Ulysses', in C. Ricks (ed.), *Tennyson: A Selected Edition* (London: Longman, 1989).

Thera, Nyanaponika, *The Heart of Buddhist Meditation* [1954], ed. S. Boorstein (San Francisco: Weiser, 2014).

Thomas, Dylan, *Collected Poems* (London: Dent, 1952).

Unger, Roberto Mangabeira, *The Religion of the Future* (Cambridge, MA: Harvard University Press, 2014).

Ward, Graham, *Unbelievable* (New York: I. B. Tauris, 2014).

Waugh, Evelyn, *Decline and Fall* [1928] (London: Penguin, 2001).

—— *Scoop* [1938] (London: Penguin, 2000).

Williams, Bernard, *Shame and Necessity* (Berkeley: University of California Press, 1993).

Wittgenstein, Ludwig, *Philosophical Investigations* [*Philosophische Untersuchungen*, 1953], trans. G. E. M. Anscombe (New York: Macmillan, 1958).

—— 'A Lecture on Ethics' [1929], in *Philosophical Review* (January 1965), 3–12.

—— *Culture and Value*, ed. Georg Henrik Wright, Heikki Nyman and Alois Pichler (Oxford: Blackwell, 1998).

Wordsworth, William, *The Prelude*, ed. J. C. Maxwell (Harmondsworth: Penguin, 1988).

—— *A Critical Edition of the Major Works*, ed. S. Gill (Oxford: Oxford University Press, 2010).

Wynn, Mark, *Emotional Experience and Religious Understanding: Integrating Perception, Conception and Feeling* (Cambridge: Cambridge University Press, 2005).

Index

154   *Index*